A Mind For Business

The Secrets of how Award Winning Entrepreneur Richard Harpin built a £1 billion business

by Michael Heatley

All proceeds support young entrepreneurs

TheEnterpriseTrust.org

Foreword by Joanna Lumley

A Mind For Business

Published by The Enterprise Trust
www.TheEnterpriseTrust.org

Cover, design and typesetting by Ayd Instone, sunmakers.co.uk

Version 1.0

ISBN: 978-0-9564567-0-0

Contents

Foreword

by Joanna Lumley

I first met Richard Harpin at The Ernst & Young UK Entrepreneur Of The Year awards in 2008 – little realising that, exactly one year later, he would invite me to contribute a foreword to his life story.

It's always inspirational to find out what makes the wealth-makers of our nation tick, and by retracing his steps Richard has created a guide to those who might want to follow in his footsteps. Many of the principles will apply across the board – though he made his fortune in plumbing insurance, he started off selling Christmas trees in Newcastle – so there should be lessons for most of us to learn from in these pages.

Richard has used his Entrepreneur Of The Year status as a platform from which to launch this book. His intention to give a copy to every school in Britain can only help inspire future captains of industry. That has to be good for the country and all of us.

So, dear reader, instead of celebrating past achievements, as I did the first time I met Richard, this could be the first page of another success story – your own!

Good luck

Joanna Lumley

Introduction

The idea of putting my life into words came following my winning of Ernst & Young's UK Entrepreneur Of The Year and a desire to encourage youngsters to set up their own business or take the lessons of business achievement and apply them to other areas of life.

I decided to do it not because I wanted a biography written, or for any egotistical reason, but as a way of encouraging the next generation of entrepreneurs. I've gone into a number of schools to tell the HomeServe story, and the feedback has always been that it's inspirational, that I've managed to motivate some of the pupils to think about how they might start up businesses.

I can't possibly go into every school in the country, so this was a more time-effective way to do it – agreeing to having a book written, putting together a teacher's resource pack to go with it and helping it form part of the enterprise syllabus for secondary schools and encouraging that next generation of entrepreneurs.

But no-one succeeds by their own efforts alone. At the end of the book I've tried to pay tribute to everybody who has helped, inspired, worked for, supplied or been connected with any of my businesses for which I am most grateful. Most importantly, "behind every successful entrepreneur..." I would particularly like to thank my wife Kate for all her support and dedicate this book to her.

Enterprise has come a long way from back in the days when I was a young entrepreneur. Just look at the success of television's The Apprentice and Dragons' Den.

The important thread that seems to run all through this is that the learning never stops – you may leave school, you may leave university, but the learning carries on. It should be everybody's life-long ambition to learn something new every day. You should then get out of bed with the feeling that each day is going to be different, fulfilling and inspirational...and, in doing that, hopefully your enthusiasm will rub off on all those around you.

Success in business and success generally is more than luck or being in the right place at the right time. It is said that luck is the marriage of preparation and opportunity and I believe that, with the right attitude and a mind for business, you will recognise the opportunities as they present themselves and take advantage of them.

People who know me know that I lead by example and enthusiasm rather than by any real talent, so if any of that rubs off on the readers of this book then the project has been worthwhile.

Richard Harpin

Chapter 1

Never give up

'I put a lot of work into trying to win but the most important thing is that if you lose it's all about knowing you did everything in your power to try to win.'

It's always nice to be recognised. And when Richard Harpin took to the stage at the Grosvenor House Hotel, London on Monday 6th October 2008 he stood face to face with someone he recognised very well indeed – actress Joanna Lumley.

No, it wasn't a walk-on part in a stage version of Absolutely Fabulous, though those words certainly applied to the evening. It was The Ernst & Young UK Entrepreneur Of The Year awards, and Harpin was fortunate enough to have been announced the winner.

Fortunate, yes. But many believe you make your own luck in business, as in all walks of life. And Harpin could look back on the past one and a half decades with a certain amount of satisfaction. The hard work put into pursuing an idea had paid off. HomeServe, the company he founded in 1993, is now the world leader in providing domestic emergency cover to homeowners.

It wasn't his first awards ceremony – that came in 1984, when he was 20 and won the Make It In Business Award and was a regional finalist in the Livewire Business Competition. The prizes then had included a rent-free factory (which he didn't take up), £3,500 and a computer. Not Entrepreneur Of The Year, yet, but it was a handy few lines to have on your CV...especially as he was still at university.

As in football, the winner of the domestic Entrepreneur Of The Year goes on to compete in Europe. (How Harpin wished he could say that of his beloved Newcastle United!). So when asked for his reaction to the award, he was already thinking of the next hurdle: 'Winning was absolutely wonderful, but to represent the UK in the global awards is a real honour.'

The papers call Harpin a 'serial entrepreneur', and history bears that out. From starting up a mail-order business selling fly-tying materials to fly fishermen while still at school, he went on to take HomeServe from foundation to a market capitalisation of over £1 billion and the status of a top 200 UK listed company, with operating profits of over £100 million.

'It gives me great pleasure, he said, 'to think that many millions of householders worldwide sleep easier at nights knowing that we are just a phone-call away. Because I sincerely believe the success of HomeServe is built on the principle of putting the customer at the heart of everything we do.'

He tells two stories to illustrate why he has been blessed with an abnormal drive and will to succeed. One is positive, the other negative and both come from his childhood.

'I've always been really driven, from the age of about four, when we lived in a little cul-de-sac in Huddersfield in West Yorkshire. My father would put me on his shoulders and look over at a helicopter landing in a nearby garden, and I thought, "I want one of those one day". I found out later it belonged to Lord Hanson, the late industrialist, who was flying in to have Sunday lunch with his parents who lived in the big house at the end of the road.

'Since then I've learned to fly fixed-wing and rotary-wing aircraft and use a helicopter most working days to get back to my family home in Yorkshire from wherever I've been.

'There's another story I always tell when people ask when I first felt an entrepreneurial spirit within me. It was the opening of the Huddersfield Ship Canal, which had been derelict. British Waterways had spent a lot of money opening it up to pleasure-boating; I must have been about four. My brother, mother and I went down to the canal to get the free boat ride that had been advertised and they said "Oh no, you're too late. Everybody's had their boat rides. Try the other side of the canal." So we walked all the way to the other side and again it was "You're too late. No boat rides."

'Don't ask me why, but it was a massive disappointment at the time. It was a fairly trivial thing, but it has really driven me. I somehow felt, even at that age, that, had I been a bit older, I'd have persuaded them to give me my free boat ride. I wanted to make sure I was successful enough to be able to get the boat ride. And I thought "I don't want my children to experience that kind of disappointment." That's no reflection on my mother, who has been a massive influence on my life,' he stresses, 'or my late father.'

So the positive combination of Lord Hanson's helicopter flying in and the negative one of providing for his family-to-be planted the entrepreneurial seed within Richard Harpin. 'I've come to believe half of it is genotype, the raw material you're born with, and half of it is phenotype – seeing the helicopter, the ship canal-experience. The magical combination of those experiences somehow turned me into the dreadful creature I am now!' Admittedly you can't choose your parents, but you can take advantage of every opportunity that comes your way.

If there is a key to everything Richard Harpin has achieved, it is that you should never give up. His Newcastle-based friend Geoff Gillie tells a story that, in a small way, demonstrates this total determination. 'We were in our late twenties and had been on a golfing holiday in Spain. We were getting a late flight back to Newcastle, so were out of the hotel by lunchtime and had all day before the flight left. We thought we'd go and have a game of golf in the afternoon, get showered and changed and then hit the town for a few drinks before getting to the airport in time to catch the flight home.

'We'd had a few beers, although nothing out of the ordinary, and were walking through the town square in Estepona when a couple of young Spanish lads came up to us and started greeting us, saying hello, shaking hands and generally being over-friendly. I immediately thought "'Uh-oh, there's going to be trouble here", but Richard hadn't picked up on this and thought they were having a bit of a laugh...

'As they were walking away, Richard suddenly realised they'd taken his wallet. Not only that, they'd got his passport as well, so all of a sudden there's a panic.' Richard was not prepared to let them go and gave chase, running after them for so long that, having stripped the wallet of money, they threw it, and his passport, on the ground just to get rid of him.

Harpin is still pretty fit one and a half decades on – and is still running just as fast for his business as ever. When in 2007 he was accepted onto the Executive Programme at Stanford University in California, with 142 MDs and chief executives from countries all over the world, a three to four-mile run kicked off every morning.

'I've never been a runner, because I've always found running a bit boring – I've done a bit on the treadmill, but never been out every morning running three or four miles. There were four groups – the ones who said "I'm not going to do this at all" even though it was expected; the walking group; the running group; and then the marathon and experienced runners'. I started in the runners' group, managed to get to the front and thought, after the first week, "I want to get up into the next group." I managed to push myself so I got up to the top eight or ten runners in the top group – I had to make myself do it.'

As for UK Entrepreneur Of The Year, he claims he'd never have voluntarily applied for a business competition. 'Somebody put me up for the one I won in 1984, and a guy called John Houlden in our mergers and acquisitions department suggested this one. He was an accountant who had always wanted to be a partner with a major accountancy firm and Ernst & Young offered him a partnership in the Birmingham office close to home.

'We kept in contact and he phoned me up one day and said "Did you know Ernst & Young do this major national business competition Entrepreneur Of The Year? I want to put you forward for it." In the same week somebody else called me, one of our external lawyers in Birmingham, saying had I considered doing Entrepreneur Of The Year? Two calls in the same week – I thought I'd better agree to do it.

'There were some great businesses competing. It was quite a long process of regional heats, with due diligence, etc. I won the regional heat and had no expectations. I always go into these things to win but I had no expectation of winning. All I did was tried as hard as I possibly could, anything I could imagine doing, to win it. There were a number of really good businesses that I thought were going to win, but I managed to go on and win the national final.

'It was fun to meet Joanna Lumley – I think she's great! I also met David Mellor for the first time, and he's good fun. Now, having won that award it would be rude not to try to capitalise on it. At the same time I was approached with the idea of my business story being written to help the next generation of entrepreneurs.

I can't possibly go to every school in the country and give a talk on my business story to motivate those secondary school 12 year-olds, to say, "Why don't you go and take a formal apprenticeship, or why don't you set up your own business?" But this is a way that I can be more time-efficient, by getting that book into every single school and promoting it by flying into some of those schools as a reward for ordering copies of it over and above the free ones I plan to pay for and send.'

Richard Harpin's achievement in taking HomeServe to the brink of the FTSE 100 in record time and, crucially, doing so with him in place as the founding CEO, has made him a headline-writer's dream. The Mail on Sunday portrayed him as 'The emergency man in a hurry. He leaps out of helicopters on skis and can't wait to turn HomeServe into a global giant.' Outstanding Company Digest described him as 'A man with enthusiasm, focus and determination beyond endurance,' while The Observer hailed 'A helicopter pilot who does nothing by halves… piloting home help to new heights.'

The Mail on Sunday felt he was a worthy Entrepreneur Of The Year. 'The 44-year-old multi-millionaire boss of HomeServe, the home repair company, founded what is the UK's 160th-biggest listed company. But somehow he still comes across as a desperately eager 25-year-old… He exhibits many characteristics one hopes to find in a multi-millionaire – dedication, attention to detail and a near-obsessive vision.'

Yet HomeServe remains a company many will not have heard of, despite the fact that it has over three million customers in Britain alone. That is because the company sells insurance policies covering almost any type of home emergency one could think of, through a wide range of partners such as nPower, Thames Water, Anglian Water, Barratt Homes, M&S and Vaillant Boilers. It is their branding that appears on the literature.

Its success is very much tied in with Harpin's personality. He is a man who leads from the front and employs the very best people to ensure his vision is delivered. Simon Blunt, a man who helped Harpin out of a tight spot when a pre-HomeServe business ran into a cash-flow problem, describes him as 'incredibly hard-working, I've only ever met two people who do the sort of hours he can do… You have to have massive amounts of stamina at his level, and he certainly has. He'll never ease off! I go skiing with him every year, and I always ask him if he's any intention of slowing down, but he's committed to getting the company into the FTSE100. He wants it to go across the world… I think he'd be totally and utterly bored if he wasn't running HomeServe.

'He has a family life, and that's definitely important to him. He's got the helicopter, and I know he's always wanted a helicopter, but one of the main reasons he likes to have it is that he can get home quickly to put the kids to bed. If ever there was someone who's got it made, it's Richard. He's got a lovely wife, three lovely children, and a phenomenally successful business…'

Blunt insists his friend has a remarkable lack of ego. 'When you meet Richard he's never boastful, and you'd never know he's achieved so much because he's remained very down-to-earth. He's always interested in people – if he meets someone, he'll want to know more about them, and he'll fire loads of questions at them –

that's something he's never lost. He's not one of these people who become full of their own self-importance.'

Rachael Hughes, Harpin's one-time flatmate who heads HomeServe's Continental European operations, believes 'Richard was born with the ability to see where a profit lies… he can smell it.' She identifies a number of values that are really important throughout the company and reflect its founder.

'You need to be energetic, dynamic, open-minded, adaptable and willing to meet a challenge, but you also need to be disciplined and rigorous. I think it's vital that all this is underpinned by some rock-solid values of respect, and realising that this is a business that works because of its people.'

Simon Blunt concurs that a secret of Harpin's success is surrounding himself with very good people. 'I remember him telling me on a skiing holiday that he was planning to get rid of someone – a quite senior person – because he wasn't challenging him enough. Richard likes to be challenged.

He's got no ego... That's another thing entrepreneurs eventually get, the ones that build up big businesses, and they eventually damage themselves because of their egos, but Richard has no ego whatsoever. He's driven by increasing the share price and the long-term profits of the company.'

Brother Stephen describes Richard as 'incredibly emotionally resilient... He has an absolute belief that it's all going to work – if it's not working, he'll try it a different way and keep trying until it does, or until he decides it's not going to, and then he'll just stop it...then immediately move on to something else. There's never a gap in the middle that I can remember, where he's thinking about what to do next – it was just on to the next thing.'

The seemingly boundless energy appears to run in the family as mother Philippa, in her eighth decade but still very active, confirms. 'He does have that energy...I don't want to say too much about myself, because this isn't about me, but I am reputed to be very energetic, and I do remember my secretary, who was about 25 years younger than me, saying "It's all right for you, you don't get tired..." It's probably in the genes, because my mother was very much that way. She was extraordinarily energetic, and I think both my sisters and my brother are, too. My brother is three years older than me, and he's still working...

'We are an energetic family, we do work long hours and put a lot into whatever we may be doing. I'd like to think that Richard has got quite a lot of that from me, because I've always worked every hour God gave me in the job that I did.'

The reason Richard Harpin entered World Entrepreneur Of The Year is the same as agreeing to the book. 'It's not because of prestige, it's not because of any egotistical reason. It would help my business story and the message of "work hard, be determined" get to more people. It would be more powerful if I was to be the first person from the UK to make it – somebody must win from the UK some day, and I'd like to use the award to do some good.'

In the end, it wasn't to be. Richard missed out on the overall title to Cao Dewang, chairman of the Fuyao Glass Industry Group, who had announced he was to donate nearly 60 per cent of his personal interest in the company to a charity foundation funding education and medical care in his native China. But the contacts Richard made will be useful in the months and years to come.

'I put a lot of work into trying to win, but the most important thing is that, if you lose, it's about knowing that you did everything in your power to try to win. Also, I thought that, had I won it, I could have done something with winning…it wasn't about the winning itself and any glory that came with it, it was the fact that if I won, that would help the distribution of my business story which, in turn, would help more young entrepreneurs get into business.

'It would have helped launch an Entrepreneurs badge in the Scouting Association in 200 countries, not just the UK, getting to 28 million Cub Scouts and so on… It was more disappointing from that point of view. I never thought I'd be UK Entrepreneur Of The Year, let alone World Entrepreneur, so it's more about how it could've helped me to help others. I did have a "How can we 42 entrepreneurs from around the world help others?" pack put into every hotel bedroom, though…'

The disappointment didn't last long, and that did not surprise mother Philippa, one of the first to get the news by telephone. 'He doesn't get disheartened, and I do remember that, when he was a child, if something had gone wrong he wanted to talk about it for five minutes. Than the subject was closed and forgotten about. He'd face it at the time and then put it behind him.

'He was quite disappointed he didn't win the Global Entrepreneur Of The Year… But once he'd told me, as far as he was concerned, the subject was closed. He wanted to talk about it, but only for a few minutes and then "That was yesterday, we're starting on something new today." He doesn't dwell on things that have gone wrong…'

Richard rated his most impressive rival as US entry Red Hat, a big operation that distributes game software, and doesn't think the British stand up well against the other nations. 'We've still never won it, which is a bit of a shame because I think there are a lot of good entrepreneurs in the UK, and the UK is Ernst & Young's second largest country in terms of size and billing income.'

Realising HomeServe's trademark red van was a recognition feature, he told his driver, 'Congratulations, Alan, I've got you a new vehicle. He was thinking I'd got one of those flash limousines like Lord Sugar, one of those big Rollers, but actually he was off to Monte Carlo for four days in a van! That worked really well. Everyone saw it parked outside the Hotel de Paris and the casino, and there aren't many red or white vans driving round Monte Carlo – the average car out there is a Bentley convertible!'

'A lot of the people there went for the fun of the four days. They were just happy to win their country's event and had no expectations of anything more. They didn't rehearse their interview, or go out of the way on any of the press stuff. I did…and although I didn't go there expecting to win, I went there intending to give it my best shot.'

Harpin debated whether he should wear a HomeServe engineer's uniform – and did. 'I don't know how that went down, but I thought it was the right thing to do.' He claimed he was very nearly late for the judging because he'd been stopped four times on his way down the corridor by people who'd got problems with the plumbing in their bathroom! 'They said no props, so I thought I'd better not take a toolbox, just a spanner. And I managed to get hold of some boot covers the HomeServe engineers wear before they step on anybody's carpet.

'At the end of the interview, I told the judges I made no apologies for coming in my engineer's outfit and not my suit because we should remember that this is the experience that our customers have. The moment of truth for our service is the moment that engineer steps over their threshold when they've got a plumbing emergency and there's water pouring through the ceiling, and that engineer is there to sort things out in their hour of need. That customer could have been paying their annual subscription for four or five years, this is the first time they've used the service. They want to know that it's good, that he's a proper engineer, he's in his uniform and he's put his boot covers on…

'We're only as good as our worst sub-contractor, our worst branch, their worst plumber on his worst day. It was really important to me to get the judges focused on this moment of truth for the customers, to understand that this is what it's all about. So when I got to the end of that and the other press interviews and stuff and I had to take off my HomeServe uniform and hand back my spanner, it was a bit of a wrench…

'I think there should have been more than one winner with different categories, as there were in the regional finals and the UK final. There should have been a social winner, and an innovator and one for entrepreneurial spirit… If they did that, they'd get more out of it, they'd get more of the people who put their heart and soul into it to go away saying "I'm going to use that to do some real good". I'm still going to do what I said I was going to do in terms of the Scouts' Entrepreneur's badge, and make sure this book has as wide a distribution as possible to encourage young entrepreneurs.

'Ernst & Young looked after everybody extremely well, showed great generosity and put their heart and soul into running the awards. Hopefully all the feedback I thought through and discussed with the other country winners will have been constructive and help to make the awards even better next year.'

Richard Harpin believes in self-improvement too and is an avid reader of business biographies. 'I prefer the "story" books because they tell a story, have a bit of a laugh and there's a useful business message – and if you can learn just one thing from every business biography you read and store it away until you need it, those tips can come in really useful. I scribble furiously in the back of every one – whenever I get the chance to read a book, lying on the beach for a couple of hours for example, I look at these ideas and think how can I apply that to my business, how can I store that nugget of wisdom. One day I'm going to be in a business situation where that will be useful...and that's someone else's experience that I've picked up for free.'

He is a great believer in looking at parallel businesses, parallel markets, and copying the things that were done in that other market, adapting them and applying them to the market in which he operates.

Those he admires include Bill Gates, 'because he invented a market, had a very clever business model, working with IBM and MS-DOS etc. and because he's always developing. I like the "Version 1.1" approach – it's not about developing something that's absolutely extraordinary, it's actually about getting it 80 per cent right, getting it into the market, and then learning and improving it. I think it's really good to say "We're launching Version 1.1, and we'll get to

Version 6.3", but don't wait until it's Version 6.3 before you launch it because you won't get the experience, your customers won't get the experience, and it's better to get it out there and then test and learn to improve.'

Richard Branson is another role model. 'I would say that the way he's developed the Virgin brand, and taken it into a number of sectors, has been inspirational. Not all of these ventures have been successful, many have failed, but he has a worldwide brand that's probably bigger than the company or the amount of money he makes. He's passionate, he's visionary and he enjoys himself.

'I've a lot of admiration for Lord Sugar, as he now is… I think he's done an even better job on The Apprentice than Donald Trump did on the original American version, and that's an inspiration to a lot of people. I think the audience for The Apprentice and Dragon's Den are probably a lot younger than a lot of people think, and I understand they've just agreed to do children's versions of both of those programmes.'

Last but not least, Harpin cites hi-fi retail guru Julian Richer and his book The Richer Way as an inspiration and role model for his own story. 'There were a lot of useful things to learn in there, but there's not a great deal of ego. He'd taken a niche market and sold more product per square foot by value than any other retailer in the UK. I met him recently and he tells me he's sold 50,000 copies of his book – it's in its fifth reprint.'

The book you're reading now may have not been Harpin's idea, but mother Philippa – still a role model –was influential in changing it from a ghostwritten autobiography to a third-person narrative. 'The important thing,' she told the author, 'and I'm sure Richard would say the same, is that it shouldn't make him sound conceited. In an autobiography, anything that's said is going to sound conceited…

'Perhaps you could suggest to him that it should be a biography, and tell him that his mother's a bit worried that otherwise it'll sound conceited? I'm not interfering – I learned a long time ago that we don't interfere – but I wonder if it's easier not to sound conceited when someone else is writing it.'

Richard Harpin may be a multi-millionaire entrepreneur with a workforce of thousands at his beck and call, but it's somehow reassuring to find that mother still knows best!

Chapter 2

Every no is really a yes

'It shows, as it had done before and would later in life, that persistence pays – you've got to knock that door down!'

Richard Harpin comes from a family of businesspeople – his parents, their brothers and sisters and their families are also entrepreneurial. So maybe there's a general genetic make-up. 'One set up his own technology firm which he sold, and his sister is married to a guy who works in business – they live in the States, where they're importing bathroom products from China and retailing them…that's my mother's sister's family, and we are very close to them.

'I have one younger brother called Stephen. We always used to think we were very different but actually we're more similar than we thought. The age difference is just over two years, but I don't think we were competitive – we felt we were very different and therefore had different interests. We used to fight a bit as brothers do but I don't think there was ever any real competition. He was more handsome than me, more intelligent than me...but I was the hard-working one!'

Richard's parents were both Yorkshire born and bred. His father, David, was also from an entrepreneurial background as his father and grandfather were cloth merchants in West Yorkshire who lost all their money in the Great Depression of 1929. David would have liked to have set up his own business, but because of their traumatic experience, his parents felt that security should be the priority. Their business failed because they weren't paid what they were due, leading to them losing everything, including their house, to pay their debts. These were the days, when for some people, bankruptcy wasn't an option.

As Stephen recalls, 'Our father saw his parents go from a comfortable life to nothing, and that made him see the risks fairly clearly... The other thing he did, every time an opportunity arose, and even when he was working for the Civil Service, when he was offered promotions, he always put us first and always turned them down – we were always doing something at school, so we couldn't move from the school or something like that. I think my father was generally a frustrated entrepreneur; he'd seen misfortune and the implications it could have if you come from an environment where if you were let down, you held your head high and did not pass on the debts to others.

'He was a terribly honourable gentleman who would have paid all his debts... unlike today, where people plunge into administration without real problems... He always put us first, which was wonderful, and I hope – in fact, I'm sure – that some of that has rubbed off on to Richard and myself.'

Father's parents understandably drummed into him that he should take a safe career so he ended up a chartered surveyor in the Civil Service. He left school at 15 without qualifications and worked hard at night school to qualify as a chartered surveyor, having worked in auction rooms as a porter holding up the antique furniture – later in life, antique collecting became David's big passion. He did well as a chartered surveyor but put his family before his career and, as already mentioned, turned down promotions which meant he would have to go to other parts of the country. He made one move from Huddersfield to Northumberland in 1969, when Richard was five, and turned down promotions after that, insisting that the family remained in Northumberland. And there they stayed until his death a couple of years ago.

'My father was the shrewd one with money,' Richard remembers, 'and did well collecting antiques – he always negotiated every piece! I got my negotiating skills from him'. Stephen agrees: 'My family are from Yorkshire, and being from Yorkshire, we talk about money. Our father was a very canny bloke, a gentleman, but he would negotiate brilliantly…he would negotiate over something that was worth, say, £40, and he would negotiate in a wonderfully clever way over months and he'd always get what he wanted. He knew before he started exactly what he was going to pay, and he'd just work at it… Every "No" was going to be a "Yes", it was just a matter of time. I'm sure I've heard Richard say that – every "No" is really a "Yes", but the other person just doesn't know it yet.'But multi-tasking is something Richard is sure he inherited from his mother, Philippa. 'She's second to none in terms of doing lots of stuff. She's the oldest Akela in the country; she's gone back to running Cub Scouts. She did that when I was young; my brother and I were cubs. She went back to it 15 years ago and is still doing it. You need a special dispensation to be able to run Cub Scouts if you're over 65. She's now 70 and is the oldest one in the country.'

His mother's family were also entrepreneurs, but their first business failed. They were shoddy manure suppliers, shipping waste cotton, which had been broken down, from the Yorkshire mills to hop farms in Kent and so on, where it was used as manure. Unfortunately, it all went wrong after they invested in a fleet of lorries just as the bottom was dropping out of the market. But Philippa's mother, Richard's grandmother, was very entrepreneurial, and she started up what proved to be a fairly successful florist's business in Yorkshire, as well as making substantial investments in property in West Yorkshire.

Philippa went to Christ's Hospital on a scholarship. Her parents certainly wouldn't have been able to afford something like that – they weren't wealthy, they were just a normal family from Yorkshire. Over the years, she has done many things that haven't strictly been business – she has written a number of books, was national adviser to the Muscular Dystrophy Group, the charity that advises sufferers on how to adapt their homes, and also got involved in fundraising – but when it comes to making things happen, getting on with things and keeping many balls in the air at the same time, Richard inherited those skills from her.

Stephen concurs: 'It's difficult to describe my mother – she's in her seventies now, a relatively small woman with a bit of osteoporosis, and stoops slightly, but she's always had – and still has – a fundamental belief that if somebody comes up with a good idea, you should absolutely do it. She has masses of enthusiasm, and never sees any problem, hurdle, barrier, in her way to stop her achieving it. When we were children, we'd go to the Cub pack, she ran it and helped to grow it, to make it the best – now she's retired and in her seventies, she's running the Cub pack again because it only had eight people in it, and she thought that was a terrible shame… the rules were that you couldn't be Akela of the Cub pack if you were over 65, so she got them to change the rules! And now there's a Cub pack with a waiting list of 30 people…

'When we were young and she wanted us all to go to church, she thought that church was a bit dead for young people, so she started up a church youth group and ran it and got a pool table in… Lo and behold, within ten minutes you've got 22 youngsters counting up their paper-round money on a Sunday in the back row of the church… When she was an occupational therapist for the Muscular Dystrophy Group, she dedicated her life to helping disabled people, and she would work very long hours trying to help these families. She found out that they didn't have enough money for wheelchairs, so her attitude was "Well I'll go and raise some…"

'And it wasn't the normal way of fund-raising, like doing a sponsored walk – she called up Kevin Keegan and got Kevin Keegan's Muscular Dystrophy Team doing the Great North Run and raised £80,000 because half of Newcastle United's supporters are on the Great North Run… this is thirty years ago, so £80,000 was serious money, and she didn't go to the fundraising department to do it, she just did it off her own bat.

'With the church, now… she's seventy-something, the church quietened down, all the youngsters left, so she started a Family Service where they get sixty people instead of the twenty they got before, because all the families are turning up now. She used to go out, in her seventies, leafleting outside school to get people in – she has an endless belief in everything…'

Richard benefited from his mother's belief when he told her he wanted to set up a business: "Fine, great idea, let's do it,' she said. ' Here's £100 I'll lend you'. And, at the age of 16, his career as an entrepreneur was up and running, although this wasn't his first business venture…

Stephen cites an essay Richard wrote at school as the first evidence of him being a budding businessman. Referred to as 'the rabbit story', it's easy to see from Stephen's description why it caused so much hilarity when it was brought out and displayed at Richard's 40th birthday party: 'It's a classic! My mother kept it... I don't know how old he was, maybe around six or seven or so, but they were asked to write an essay about their pets, so everybody turns up with an essay about how cuddly Flopsy is, or whatever, but Richard's was absolutely beyond belief... It went something like "I have twelve rabbits, Flopsy, Mopsy, Topsy... Flopsy is worth 2p, Mopsy is worth 4p, Topsy has just had 12 babies, each of which can be sold for 1p..." I mean, unbelievable... he was breeding rabbits at the time and selling them to people, but I don't know where that came from at such a young age. Must be genetics, somehow... '

Livestock aside, the career of Richard Harpin the entrepreneur started at the Royal Grammar School in Newcastle where, in the first or second year, at about 12 years of age, he ran a tuck shop from his locker, going to the cash and carry and selling sweets and stuff to classmates. But although there are few things closer to a schoolboy's heart than sweets, Richard found one in the playground game of conkers; this was to be his next venture.

Lots of the RGS pupils lived in the centre of Newcastle, whereas Richard lived in a small village where there were lots of horse chestnut trees. He sent his mates up the trees to shake them and get all the conkers down – it was much more effective than throwing sticks up or waiting until the conkers fell because then it was too late in the season and everyone had got them.

They shook the branches, collected the conkers, graded them and put them in plastic bags. These were then labelled and priced and sold on to distributors who would sell them individually to other people.

Richard's education had started a hundred miles away at the Mount School in Huddersfield. 'I used to walk to school, he recalls. 'We went back a few months ago and my wife, Kate, couldn't believe a four year-old would be allowed to walk a mile to school alone by the side of a main road, but I remember doing that. I also remember doing the walk in reverse when I flicked a pea across the canteen at lunchtime and got sent home for the rest of the day! It was a lonely walk thinking of ways to explain to my mother why I'd been sent home.

'I was only at the Mount for a year before we moved up to Northumberland. I went to a private school, then the local primary school – probably because it was the closest – and, at ten, went to the middle school that had just opened. A year later I took the entrance exams for the two top independent schools in Newcastle, the RGS and Dame Allan's. They were about 16 miles away from home.

'I won a scholarship to Dame Allan's, which would have been a great help to my parents as it covered a reasonable amount of the school fees. I didn't manage to get a scholarship to its rival, the Royal Grammar School, but we felt it was the better school. My brother ended up going there as well, and I enjoyed my time. The choice for my parents was either holidays aboard or educating their sons privately. They chose the latter.' (The lack of holidays was ironic since Richard's godfather, Derek Bamforth, made his fortune from saucy Blackpool-style cartoon postcards.)

Stephen agrees their parents made the right decision: 'With our father a Civil Servant, and mother going to work as an Occupational therapist, these were not particularly well-paid jobs. The poshest holiday we ever went on over the age of six was a caravanning holiday... I can't remember my parents ever spending anything on what you'd consider an extravagance or a luxury. They put all the money, and all of the time, into sending us to a decent school. It was a huge sacrifice... it was very good of them.'

At first it didn't seem they'd make a great return on their investment. Academically Richard was only ever average at the Royal Grammar School, although it was full of pretty bright pupils. He remembers his French teacher saying 'Richard is the hardest working and most conscientious person in the whole class but he's going to fail his French O Level.' He was wrong because Richard made sure he passed, but he always had to work hard.

'I remember my mother having a conversation with one of our teachers and hearing "how Richard had been doing in his chemistry lessons". Having heard all the bad things, she thought she should stick up for me and said "He's going to be a millionaire before you are!" The teacher laughed and said "I have absolutely no doubt you're right, Mrs Harpin. He's always late for my lessons because he's been to the bank, or seeing some potential business client ..."

> 'I think it's very important for everybody at school to have a really good grasp of being able to write properly, because if you're in business you have got to be able to set out your thoughts in writing in a cohesive manner. It's obviously important to be numerate, too.

I wouldn't say I particularly enjoyed maths, but I had a good grasp of business things. I always do a financial calculation on the back of an envelope to see if something's going to stack up, so you've got to feel comfortable on both of those. I quite enjoyed history as an 11 year-old but that interest then developed into Economics.'

His GCE O level results – two As, two Bs and five Cs – were a bit of a disappointment. Looking back, Richard accepts that he might have done better academically if it hadn't been for his outside interests, but he remains convinced that it was a good sacrifice to make. (For younger readers, GCEs were the forerunner of the GCSE system.)

He recalls not being particularly into sport in those days because 'it was all running and rugby'. He did a bit of rugby outside of school but didn't particularly like school sports. Instead, as his chemistry master was all too aware, he used to be off talking to the bank manager because the bank was close to the school and he had money to pay in from the business he'd been running.

And, curiously enough, that business was sports-related. They say that angling is a hobby that can take over your life. In Richard's case, it not only did that but also filled his parents' home with feathers, hooks, vices, catalogues and all manner of paraphernalia for several years. Fly-fishing for trout and salmon was the game, and profit, rather than pleasure, was the aim.

The all-important item the anglers needed was a fly, a lure that encouraged fish to come up to the surface and, by trying to feed on the 'fly', end up on the angler's hook. The lure had to be realistic enough to fool the fish, and this was achieved by tying feathers together. Now fly-tying, to some anglers, is a pleasure. To others it's a bind – and that's not a technical term! So taking that chore away was worth money to them. The three years from 1978 saw Richard tying flies and selling them to friends, tackle shops and at village shows. His target audience was people who preferred to buy the completed flies rather than spend the time putting them together themselves.

And time, in this case, was the valuable resource. By 1981 his lines of supply of raw material were such that it made sense to sell them to fly-tyers like himself rather than go for the ready-made market. Fly-Tying Tackle Products was born.

Richard recalls how it all developed: 'I'd started tying flies at home at the age of eight or nine because it was more fun than doing Airfix model kits. I had a friend, Nick Whitehouse, who was a fly fisherman and tied his own flies. I had no interest in fishing myself, it was far too boring, but I was interested in tying flies. And that presented me with a business opportunity.

'Other mail order firms I'd dealt with had given me poor service, often advertising items that were out of stock due to insufficient stock levels and charging what I considered uncompetitive prices. Naturally, I aimed to make Fly-Tying Tackle Products leaders in the field, offering a return-of-post service. First year turnover just exceeded £1,500, of which £356 was profit. So far, so good.

Richard moved from tying to wholesaling when he realised that, by buying the materials from the fishing tackle shop locally, tying them up and selling them back, the shop was winning twice. It was making money selling him the stuff and then getting the flies at a discount. 'They were taking advantage of me as a schoolchild,' he reflects, 'So I said I'm not having this! I'll cut them out, get my own materials and cut the retailer out. Then I discovered they were so cheap I could sell them on to other people.'

To test the waters, he placed a small ad of just 20 words in Trout And Salmon, the sport's monthly magazine. It cost eight pounds to enter this under the fly-tying column in the classifieds. At this point he hadn't even set up the business – it was simply a test to see how many people would respond. Enough people called to convince him that he should set it up, print a little catalogue, put shelves up in his bedroom and start up the business with his mother's hundred quid.

QUALI-TYE
BRAND
PEACOCK
FLY-TYING TACKLE PRODUCTS

The best flies are made from cockerel's capes, stiff feathers from cockerels used to make the fly stand up on top of the water, and the quality of these is really important. At first, he imported them from India a few thousand at a time, but they had to be sent to Rentokil to be fumigated to get rid of the bugs. He decided that cost too much money, so he obtained an old chest freezer, bought his own formaldehyde, masks and white coats and did his own fumigation.

His first experience of proper retail was the National Game Fair which took place over three days every year, attracting some 150,000 visitors from the hunting, shooting and fishing set. Retailers could buy a bit of a marquee for the three days, 30 feet front to back with a 15-foot frontage. It cost £1500 for the three days which was quite a bit of money the first time he did it aged 15 or 16, but it proved to be very valuable experience.

Brother Stephen was his trusted lieutenant: 'We used to hire a white Transit van every year (the first year Richard had to get an older friend to drive), and we'd gather together all this stuff and put it in the van, then drive it down to the fair. We'd camp in a farmer's field on the way, have a few tins of beer and smoke cigarettes!

'I remember being terribly well-organised – there'd be loss-leaders, and not-quite-loss-leaders at the front of the stand, and we worked out in about five minutes that if you were standing out in front of the stand you'd sell five times as much as if you were behind the stand... It was a great trading environment, like being a market trader... Our parents came, and they brought the caravan... it was like a holiday for them! Our father would stand at the back, with a tin of beer, assessing everything, and mother would be down the front, with her massive enthusiasm.'

'It was a great learning experience,' Richard agrees. 'You had the face-to-face contact with the customers which I didn't have by selling via mail order. I learnt that you had to be very organised – price everything you have, and have everything on display boards. Then you had to have shopping baskets – those little blue mushroom baskets. Customers get a basket, fill it up, come to the counter and we tot it all up. We had big calculators, bags, special offer boards…'

Over those three years they managed to double the sales each year. Richard looked at the name and decided that Quali-Tye was much more distinctive than Fly-Tying Tackle Products, and each year they improved the labelling, had better staffing and so on. Continuous refinement was the key – but it was a chance remark overheard on the third year of running the stand that presented him with another opportunity.

'A few of the wives and girlfriends of fishermen looked at the big purple flies with an ostrich feather built in and said "Oooh! They'd make nice earrings…" That was the extent of my market research! I set up a business in parallel with the flies and, in rather un-PC fashion, called it Hookers.'

By that time Philippa was looking after the mail-order fishing tackle business, run from home with a couple of part-time employees. It had moved out of Richard's bedroom and into an outbuilding. Richard had a load of outworkers in York. He went around on a bicycle delivering them the kidney wires to put on the hooks. Then they put them into bags, put labels on and put them onto display cards ready for delivery to the shops and hair salons.

The idea was that hair salons might put a card of the earrings next to their till, encouraging impulse buys.

And this was Richard's opportunity to make his mark further afield – in the nation's capital, no less. Stephen remembers Richard 'calling all the big department stores in Newcastle and London. To the London ones, he'd say "I'm coming down on Tuesday 22nd to see Harrods, and I wonder if I could pop in and see you as well?" – and of course he saw them... And they took these cards – he had a card made, they were called Hookers Earrings, and poor old Stephanie a girl who lived in the village agreed to be the hooker. We had these flies made in Mauritius, and of course they came with a barb on them, and they had a ring in the top of them, so we sat there with wire cutters, cutting the barb off them, to flog to John Lewis. Absolutely marvellous!

'I was chief salesman, so I used to punt them round Leazes Arcade in Newcastle and sell them to the traders at £18 a card. Richard really got his teeth stuck into that one. I'm really not sure whether he liked making money, or just liked being in business...'

'Actually,' Richard admits, 'I quite enjoyed the publicity too! After Christmas sales had exceeded expectations, Stephanie and I found our picture in The Sun newspaper in January 1985...' The news item beside it read:

'Businessman Richard Harpin is hoping to net a fortune by selling fishing flies as earrings. And Richard, who runs a mail-order fishing tackle firm, says girls on Tyneside are falling hook, line and sinker for the multi-coloured jewellery, priced at £1.95. He got the idea from women visitors at a fishing exhibition who said the flies would make attractive and unusual earrings. Now Richard, 20, from Northumberland, hopes to sell them nationwide.'

The venture also propelled Richard onto television programmes, thanks to a risqué press release headed 'Hookers to hit the high streets.' Richard is certain they will one day come back in fashion...though this is possibly wishful thinking, given that 15,000 pairs are stored somewhere in a Newcastle rental property he owns. Maybe someone will one day find them!

Richard finds that Stephanie Golightly is just one of the girls hooked on his line in earrings.

Hooked on fashion!

WHEN young entrepreneur Richard Harpin was fishing around for ways to develop his fly-tying business, he came up with the idea of turning the flies into fashion earrings.

He was only 16 when he started in business, importing and exporting feathers and flies to fly-tyers and fishermen.

Now 20, Richard, who runs the mail order fly-tying from his home in Cadehill Road, Stocksfield, Northumberland, decided on the new veriation while exhibiting at the National Game Fair in Hampshire last July.

The winner of last year's Make It In Business aware and regional winner in the Livewire business competition explained: "The wives and girlfriends of fishermen visiting the fair all commented that my flies would make attractive earrings.

"The idea just took off from there. My market research in the North-East has proved so encouraging with a take-up of the earrings in hair salons, boutiques and craft shops, with many repeat orders that I now feel confident in launching the product nationally."

Although he was now at university, Richard had no intention of leaving his business interests in anyone else's hands. In these long-ago, pre-mobile phone days, he had to be contactable at all times. Not only did he have big trade customers from the fly-tying industry who needed to make decisions calling him, his mother needed to get hold of him if they'd had a particular order coming in and they needed advice. And, of course, there was now also the earring business.

'So I got a landline put in with an answerphone, the only person ever to have one in the history of York University. A mile of virgin cable had to be laid, and I was the only student at a British hall of residence to have a landline of their own. Fortunately it was a fixed price of forty pounds, as I recall, so I fear British Telecom made a loss on that one…'

Richard had taken his A Levels in Economics, Geography and History, obtaining an A in Economics – his favourite, needless to say – and two Ds. Unfortunately it wasn't a good enough combination to get into either his first or second choice of University, York and Hull respectively. York required B-C-D – the right number of points but not the B-C-D specified. And Hull wanted ten points, not the nine (five and two twos) he had achieved.

'I rang York and said "I want to come down and see you because I think you're a great university and I've got a lot to add. I'm going to get involved in extra-curricular activities, Economics I excel at, please take me." They said "We'll let you know – don't call us…"

'That would have been it for most people. Not me! I got on the next train down to York, knocked on the admissions officer's door, went to see the head of faculty of the Economics Department. They were over-subscribed but I managed to get in. It shows, as it had done before and would later in life, that persistence pays – you've got to knock that door down!'

They say University is the time of your life, and Richard certainly played hard as well as worked hard. He was entertainments officer of Wentworth College and on the committee organising all the bands in the central hall. At Wentworth they couldn't afford bands as they weren't a big enough venue, so they had to have exciting events that cost no money to put on. Of course, that was a challenge Richard was keen to meet.

'We came up with the idea of replicating Cilla Black's Blind Date TV programme,' he remembers. 'It was the biggest success in the history of the University. We got all the celebrity students to take part and there was no cost to put it on. Then I got involved in the University entertainments committee. Bob Geldof and his Boomtown Rats came, but he left empty-handed because he incited the audience to stand up.

'We didn't pay him his three thousand pound fee and we couldn't use the venue for quite a while afterwards because the university authorities said "If you're having stand-up bands we can't insure you." My friend Nick Duxbury was particularly impressed we'd called the future Live Aid supremo's bluff, being as we were only in our early 20s. Some bands used to cancel if they got to Number 1 in the charts the week they were going to play. Paul Young was one, Men At Work (one-hit wonders of 'Down Under' fame) another. We had very little recourse. Bands feigned illness but we knew they didn't want to come to York when they were moving up the chart. It was good experience though, and I learned a lot from that.'

On a more business-oriented front, Richard was also on the committee that ran the Industrial Society, which gave him a good insight into how some businesses are run. His Economics degree covered all the usual ground – macroeconomics, microeconomics, laws of supply and demand and elasticity of price. But, as an adjunct to his degree course, Richard was interested in getting out and getting some proper experience. In particular, he wanted to study Giffen goods – the higher the price, the more people will pay.

'I attempted a study of manufacturing businesses in Newton Aycliffe in Durham,' he recalls. 'My question was "How do you determine price?" And every single one of them said "We buy at this price, we add on a mark-up and sell at this price' – in other words, cost plus. I just put it in my head that I wanted a business where the selling price was not related to the purchase price. Luckily I got my consumer marketing training at Procter and Gamble and that very much said "Don't charge a price based on what you pay for it, but what the consumer is prepared to pay."

'It's the value equation. Hopefully you've got a product that's such good value it's exactly what people want. Ideally, the cost of you providing the product or service is relatively small but it's got a high end value. Hence the peace of mind with the HomeServe model, as you will discover.'

After university, Richard ended up selling the fly-tying business to his main trade customer. As well as selling direct, he also supplied tackle shops, and there was one close by that said they'd make an offer for the business, so he had the business and the stock valued and the deal was done. He'd learned a great deal from running Quali-Tye, but having finished university he was keen to get on to something new. At this stage, he had no idea what the 'Big Idea' might be, but it was logical to sell up, bank a bit of money, and move on.

His first serious business venture had been quite an experience, and had made him friends as well as money. As Stephen remembers, Richard had flies made in Nakuru, Kenya, by a man named Charles Thuku, and at the time not many people were importing from there: 'I've got no idea how he found the bloke who made the flies, but he used to get these letters that said: "I praise the Lord for your business… I pray to God that you may send me money soon"…'

True to form, Richard kept his end of the bargain and the final letter from Charles, expressing his undying thanks for changing his world, confirmed Richard's underlying business ethos of a fair rate for the job. Bob Geldof would surely have approved!

Chapter 3

Failures are just learning points along the way

'Every successful person is able to sell themselves, sell their idea. You've got to have an element of salesmanship.'

Richard's father always wanted him to become a chartered accountant, a safe profession. He knew his son wanted to be in business but insisted this was the best thing to do, and Richard reluctantly agreed. In his third year at University he got a job lined up with Deloittes in Newcastle at, he recalls, a salary of six thousand pounds a year.

'Then I saw an ad for a marketing course run by Procter & Gamble, a multinational whose product ranges run from personal care, household cleaning and laundry detergents through to prescription drugs and disposable nappies. Their brand names are among the best-known in the world.'

The course was advertised as 'Three days of fun in Newcastle in a Holiday Inn', which sounded good on paper! But, as with university, Richard had to break down a door to get in since few non-Oxbridge students were accepted. He was the only person who applied from York, and later discovered that somebody from P&G got off the train to see him only because they were passing through on their way back from the ad agency in London. 'They said "There's this maverick guy in York called Richard Harpin – I'll get off the train and see if we want him on our marketing course." I managed to persuade him, went on the course and had a great time. Being a local boy helped me make many friends there.' Among those on the course were Ben Mingay, Charles Wilson and future TV sports presenter Hazel Irvine.

At Procter & Gamble, Richard progressed to the dizzy heights of brand manager and worked on several world-famous brands including Fairy Liquid and Camay and one not very famous, Vortex bleach, in three and a half years between 1986 and 1990. He recalls having broken up with a girlfriend who later complained she thought of him every time she did the washing up and saw the iconic Fairy Liquid bottle!

It was a great learning experience and gave the young entrepreneur a solid grounding in marketing and how to see things from a consumer point of view. His contemporaries included Chris de Lapuente, who went on to head the UK organisation and now has a worldwide category role, and Mike Clasper, now chairman of HM Revenue & Customs.

Interestingly, his brother Stephen later followed him into the company, albeit down South. This is his perspective on the P&G experience: 'I think it's very good training at that young age. In two ways in particular. One is discipline in communication. Procter &

Gamble were very anal about it – well, I say anal, but I think it was a good discipline – and everything had to be on one page, getting it on one page communicates it properly.

'Secondly I would say the principles of marketing were learned very quickly because that was the core expertise of the company, and I learned them in an extraordinarily structured way which, even 20 years since my marketing career, I still remember. It was a great company for that, and I'm sure Richard's success is partially to do with the skills he picked up there.

'I got into marketing after chatting it through with Richard. If you're going to be in business, you've got a chance of doing well if you know marketing or finance. Finance seemed a bit complicated to me…so we're kind of similar.'

Having an entrepreneurial character, the opportunity to go and work for one of the world's most fantastic marketing companies put Richard in a very fortunate position. It meant that he had excellent blue-chip marketing training, he was able to earn his stripes, and it taught him to think that you always run a business with the end-consumer in mind. How do you set your price? You ask the customer what they'll pay, rather than look at what it costs to manufacture. Do it in that way and you will have a really powerful business formula and great margins.

'I think Procter & Gamble was the magic ingredient that allowed me to combine everything I'd learned from running small businesses prior to HomeServe with good blue-chip marketing training,' he reflects. 'I stayed at Procter & Gamble until I was promoted to brand manager, running my own brand, which is like running your own mini-business within a large corporation. You are very focused on driving the marketing and promotions, on pricing strategy and trial strategy and getting the customers in.'

But not everything he was doing at the time fell under the Procter & Gamble umbrella. Having not long ago been a student, he needed little persuading when a P&G colleague, Richard Johns, suggested there was a gap for a national magazine to go to all first-year 'freshers' with a guide to the town or city they'd be living in for the next three years. Johns had always wanted to put a magazine on every newsagent's shelf in the country, and the new publication was his idea. He was the editor and the creative force behind the content, while Richard provided the business expertise.

It was run from Harpin's converted garage office in Gosforth, Newcastle, where the two set up their own publishing business. They arranged wide-ranging national distribution and had a team of people selling advertising space. A lot of effort went into putting it together – not only was it a national magazine, but they attempted the impossible by putting local pub/restaurant/club guides in each, depending on where it was sold.

They took on all the major universities, found somebody to write the local guides and somebody to sell the advertising space. Finally, they had people looking after the logistics of putting the separate local guides into a national magazine and getting the right mag into the right WH Smith on the right shelf. And, against all odds, it worked!

'The main objective of mine, Harpin explains, 'having organised distribution, was to persuade advertisers to give students offers via high-value vouchers. Then, having secured them, I next had to get it into every WH Smith and John Menzies in the country. That was really ambitious but we managed to pull it off.

'It was great experience, but Connect was a one-off – it wasn't a saleable business. The other Richard achieved one of his life dreams, while I learned from doing it and stored many nuggets of experience in the back of my mind that would hold me in good stead when I found the really big idea.

One of the most important things the young Richard Harpin learned from running Connect was the value of determination. It's something he is convinced that every successful person, not just those in business, needs.

'Every successful person,' he asserts, 'is able to sell themselves, sell their idea. You've got to have an element of salesmanship. I learned that fact the hard way, sitting in my converted garage flogging advertising space to Sainsbury's, Dixons and other major national companies.

'I remember persuading John Clare – who was a marketing manager at the time, not even a marketing director let alone the chief executive of [Currys, Dixons and PC World owner] DSG International that he should put a high-value voucher in our coupon book in our student mag. That was the hardest sell I'd ever done because he'd never heard of the magazine – not surprising, as we hadn't yet published it – and never heard of me, and our contact was on the phone only. Getting through to people like that with an unproven concept of a student magazine and persuading them to buy advertising space was the hardest thing. Once you've done that, other selling becomes easier.

'When I'd sold a big magazine advertising deal to one of those national clients I knew this was it – it was going to work. It was a eureka moment I'd also have with HomeServe some five years later.'

A key figure in Richard's business ventures during those early days at Procter & Gamble was another of his colleagues there, Jeremy Middleton. Connect was, in fact, one of the few business ventures

THE STUDENT SURVIVAL GUIDE
ONLY
▸ OVER 50 PAGES
who, what, why, where, how and when
▸ FREE YEAR-PLANNER
▸ MONEY
getting it, handling it
▸ HOMEHUNTING
finding and keeping accommodation
▸ SEX & HEALTH
the ups and downs
▸ FREE COMPETITION
win a trip to Egypt or an Akai stereo
▸ INTERVIEWS
John Peel, Jon Snow and Prefab Sprout
▸ FEATURES
including sport and entertainment on a budget
▸ OVER £25 OF FREE SAVINGS VOUCHERS
alcohol, stationery, electrical goods, travel, and more
CONNECT
OVER £25 FREE VOUCHERS
ANNUAL STUDENT GUIDE 1988/89
PRICE £1.00

he undertook without Jeremy at his side. Almost everything else he did while still at P&G was done jointly with Jeremy, and the two still remain the closest of friends – they are godfathers to each other's oldest children.

Jeremy had joined Procter & Gamble a couple of years before Richard. He'd been in banking, but was not the typical banking type so he'd changed career and joined P&G. At first, Richard didn't know him particularly well, although he'd worked as part of Jeremy's brand team with Zest and Fairy Liquid, which were Richard's first products as a brand assistant; Jeremy was assistant brand manager at this point.

'You tended to mix with your peer group,' Richard recalls, 'so I didn't know him socially. But when he got an offer to go and become a P&G Marketing Manager in Egypt for a year it brought us together – and that in turn was the catalyst for us to enter the property business. He had a few houses he was letting out to young professionals on a room-by-room basis; the one he lived in, his girlfriend's house and one other he had bought.

He came and saw me and told me he needed someone to look after the houses as the person he was going to use had let him down. I said I'd take it up, negotiated a good deal and, by the time he got back from Cairo a year or so later, I'd bought three or four houses myself. I let out my own house by the room in the way he had done and that was my move into property. The only problem was trying to do the full-time Procter & Gamble job and running a property letting business.'

Jeremy remembers his first impressions of Richard: 'I was at Procter & Gamble, as assistant brand manager for Fairy Liquid. Richard came in as a brand-new sprog, in the position of brand assistant – there wasn't much difference in what we did, to be honest, but these things were very hierarchical. I didn't know him that well, but he was always extremely entrepreneurial and when we were there was always trading in various businesses...

'It was extremely unusual for people at P&G to be doing these extra-curricular things – most people who go there are graduate high-fliers, focused on getting to the top of the soap industry, as surprising as that may sound. P&G are extremely successful commercially, but it's also a great place to go to get trained in marketing and it would be unusual to do much else. Richard was one of the few who were doing other things, and I think people were happy to turn a blind eye as long as your work for the company was good and you continued to deliver. I was also one of the few other people doing other things, although he and I were doing them independently at the time.

'I should imagine that about 80 per cent of P&G employees were Oxbridge – I went to Kent University, as it happens – but what they tend to do is try to recruit people who've got something different about them, and it is quite a hard place to get into. I think he'd have got in not on the basis of his degree, but because he'd already won Young Entrepreneur Of The Year, and that would have looked distinctive to them. He may well have impressed them at the interview as being driven and so on.

'I remember he was very creative as a brand assistant – the sort of project you'd get was to come up with promotions for Fairy Liquid, and while most people would have thought in terms of money-off coupons he'd be coming up with a free magazine on the pack or something equally bizarre. He'd always be trying to think of something totally different... (Not only did Richard include a copy of Prima worth more than the liquid itself, but persuaded publishers Gruner & Jahr to bear all the costs.)

'Richard did quite well at P&G – he made it to brand manager, which is what most people aspired to, so he must've done pretty well even if he wasn't spectacular. But there are some people who start out modestly and end up doing fantastically. One of our former colleagues is currently one of the Presidents there, and he's very near the top of the company, so you can come in at the bottom and if you stick with it then you may go right to the top. That's the beauty of P&G – they don't recruit from outside. In HomeServe, even though some of the top people are headhunted some have come up through the ranks.'

For evidence of what could happen without Jeremy's wise counsel, Richard only needs to ask him to remind him about the Christmas tree project – not one of Richard's greatest business successes: 'I remember Richard was getting up at four in the morning to sell Christmas trees in pub car parks, but the greengrocers and so on who drank in the pub would ask why this lad was being allowed to sell trees in the car park… Richard had just gone big, brought in a couple of big consignments of trees, and suddenly found himself chucked off his selling sites. He was in big trouble. So what he used to do was get up at the crack of dawn and go off to do some wholesale trading before coming in and doing a full day's work at P&G. He then left to work through till midnight doing deliveries and selling them on the few sites he still had left.'

Brother Stephen has a tale to tell, too: 'I don't know whether this is a fact, or just a myth in my mind, but I'm sure I remember turning the corner of the drive, and my father slamming his brakes on because some ridiculous number of Christmas trees had been dumped on the drive…

'Richard had bought this load of Christmas trees, and the bottom had dropped out of the market. So there was a discussion about how we were going to sell them – my mother never said "How are you going to sell them?" it was always "How are we going to sell them?" with her usual enthusiasm… I think Stocksfield Scouts were recruited after a quick ring-round.

'We hired a white van and did deals with landlords and pubs in Newcastle to sell Christmas trees in their car parks, and I remember there being a hoo-ha in the Journal about unfair competition because he wasn't paying rates and so on… I think there was also a story that year about him being the only guy ever to sell 400 Christmas trees in the Bigg Market in Newcastle on Christmas Eve!'

A further flavour of Richard's complicated life back then can be gained from Geoff Gillie, Richard's best drinking pal from his Newcastle days, who now runs a shipping agency business in the city and still has a shareholding in HomeServe.

'I'm a year older than Richard, and I met him in the late Eighties, when he was just about to finish with Procter & Gamble and I was working for the family business, as I do now. I had a house on the edge of town, in an area called Jesmond, a popular suburb of Newcastle where all the youngsters hung out, drank copious amounts of beer and did all the usual stuff. I suppose I was about 25, and he was 24. He'd been at Procter & Gamble for three years or so, and was in the process of moving to Deloitte to become a management consultant.

'I met Richard through the local social scene – it was a continuous round of parties in the evenings, but he was always the one who was up bright and early in the morning doing his deals. When you listened to him talking, you thought "This guy's really going to make it big, or else he's all talk and no action." But it was pretty obvious to me that he was going to make it big, because he seemed to have this continuous motor running, and he left no stone unturned. He was just one of those people, and if you're lucky enough to meet one of them in your life you're very fortunate – a very intriguing guy...'

When Jeremy came back to the UK, the property business was booming, and it wasn't long before they'd built up quite a big portfolio. But Jeremy wasn't about to give up the day job to manage it.

'I'd come to the conclusion that I was never going to start my own soap company,' he says, 'and I wanted to come back to the UK to try to go into business. I decided to go into management consultancy, because I thought I might just end up with my own business in that area, and it was a good chance to look at other things.'

Jeremy went to work for PricewaterhouseCoopers and, with Richard still with P&G and burning the candle at both ends they needed someone to look after their properties. They placed an ad in the paper and went round to people's houses to interview them, claiming that they liked to interview people in their own homes because it gave them a better idea of them. The truth was they didn't have an office to invite them to!

It was a process that led to one or two unusual interviews, as Richard admits: 'I remember interviewing one of the candidates who lived in a massive mansion in Newcastle. We interviewed her in her husband's home office and she was on a big padded chair and we were sitting on two little stools. I've never felt so intimidated interviewing anybody in my whole life! Needless to say she didn't get the job…'

Shortly afterwards, a lady named Jane Dixon was interviewed under much more relaxed circumstances. She lived in a very pleasant flat in Jesmond, in close proximity to the Metro tube system. Richard and Jeremy thought this would be a good office and that Jane was pretty good as well, so they managed to do a deal whereby they used her home as an office and her lounge as the place where the young professionals came to see what properties were available. Their weekly meeting every Saturday morning took place around Jane's kitchen table!

The business was christened Professional Properties, a straightforward name that described exactly what it did. It was a highly successful property letting and management company that also offered a refurbishment service and investment service for those that wanted to buy properties to let. This was long before the 'buy-to-let' boom, when very few people were doing it.

Here's Jeremy's take on how things developed: 'I chatted to Richard, and we very quickly came to the conclusion that since we'd both got these extra properties, it might be a good idea to join forces and buy some more and start renting them out. So we did a deal – the deal was that we would go into business together, starting out with property, but looking for something we'd both really like to move into.

'We'd go into management consultancy – I went to PricewaterhouseCoopers and he went to Deloittes – and whatever we earned would be pooled and shared between us, including income from outside the business itself. One of us would quit management consultancy and concentrate on the business, and once it was generating enough money, the other would follow suit.

'So we started off buying property and renting it out, then we formed a letting agency so we could have people looking after the properties on our behalf. Then we started thinking about ways we could make things happen faster, so we looked at franchising… I can't remember what came first, but pretty quickly we took a

SPECIAL FEATURE

Property firm offers a 'cash free' investment service

Professional Properties are a specialist letting, management and investment firm who are offering people the chance to buy residential investment properties without spending any cash. As long as clients have a home which is worth at least £25,000 more than their mortgage, Professional Properties can help them invest the equity in their home in up market properties in Newcastle where the rental income will cover all the costs of the purchase (including finance).

As Jane Dixon, one of Professional Properties' Managers explains: "We have already helped a number of people to own an investment property. We offer clients a comprehensive service as follows:

- We find property in the best areas of Newcastle and negotiate a discount on the purchase price.
- We arrange the finance to make the investment. This is normally via a remortgage of the clients home to release unused equity, combined with a commercial mortgage to make up the balance of the funding.
- We refurbish the property as required.
- We equip the property with furniture and fittings to make it suitable for letting.
- We let the property on assured shorthold tenancy agreements to young professionals.
- We manage all aspects of the property and secure vacant possession for clients when required.

Messrs Richard Harpin and Jeremy Middleton are the two partners who originally set up Professional Properties, combining their background in property with experience in industry and management consultancy.

Mr Harpin says, "The scheme is unique because we invest in Newcastle where rental incomes are higher in relation to housing purchase costs than anywhere else in the country. This means you can cover all your costs. Additionally, if you finance the purchase through a remortgage of your existing property you will not have to inject any cash at all."

Mr Middleton is keen to highlight how easy the process is for investors. "We take away all the time consuming aspects of finding, refurbishing and managing property. This covers any crises that occur like a burgulary, leaking pipes or non-paying tenants. It also ensures that the property is well maintained and is kept in good decorative order. Levels of risk are minimal. Clients receive all the benefits of capital growth with the low level of risk associated with an asset backed investment."

The partners private prospectus shows that an investor would make £70,000 after 5 years assuming capital growth levels in line with the post war average. Investors who reinvest the surplus to purchase additional properties within the first five years get an even greater return. Surprisingly, the returns from their investment service are significantly more attractive than investing in one of the many BES assured tenancy funds. Although Business Expansion Schemes qualify for tax relief at the investors highest marginal rate, they are not 'gearing up' your investment, so returns are not as high.

Pictured left to right (back row), Mr Jeremy Middleton, Margaret Kerr, Pat Robson and Mr Richard Harpin. (Front row) Lorna Foster, Jane Dixon and Jean Charlton.

If you would like a copy of the investment prospectus, and for further information, contact Professional Properties, 20 Osborne Road, Jesmond, Newcastle upon Tyne, NE2 2AD. Telephone: (091) 212 1111.

franchise to run a mortgage broking business, and we took a retail unit in Middlesbrough. Richard was the one who was going to run it, so he quit Deloittes while I stayed on at PWC, and he would commute to and from Albert Road in Middlesbrough – not the sexiest place to be! There were various iterations of that while we tried to develop it, but it was never going to make a fortune… We'd got the letting agency, Professional Properties, up and running by this time, and out of all this came a series of other initiatives.'

As Jeremy says, that was the start. They needed maintenance people to look after the properties, which in turn led on to other things – an ironing service, the A1 Fastfix repair and maintenance business, Total Interiors interior design and decorating, mortgage shops. They tried to make some of these work for quite a long time and they'd bumble along making a little bit of money, but the problem was that they weren't really finding the 'Big Idea'.

'We steered clear of becoming estate agents,' Richard recalls. 'There was a link between estate agency and owning property, but the letting and management was the end of the property market we were interested in. We did get involved in a business called Mortgage Advice Shops which was another link with property, but we never quite made the move into estate agency, although a friend of mine, Simon Blunt from Derbyshire, whom I met at an exhibition selling Mortgage Advice Shop franchises, became the biggest estate agent in the East Midlands.'

Jeremy: 'When we first started buying houses together, we would go down Shields Road in Newcastle, in Byker, which is an area where you've got some really cheap shops, and we would take it in turns to go into these shops and try to negotiate to reduce the price of a pack of forks. We'd set a budget, and we'd each have to go out to beat the budget – it was a competition, but we were also trying to do things as cheaply as possible. He's never changed from that... he's a good buyer, and he has no nerves when it comes to negotiating.'

The plan was to buy what are called Tyneside flats – these look like terraced houses, but are actually an apartment upstairs and another downstairs. Normally the apartment downstairs had two bedrooms, while the upstairs one probably had three bedrooms. Richard hit on the idea of putting another staircase in the upstairs apartment, going into the loft, and putting another two bedrooms in there, then letting them to the young professional market. Instead of having three bedrooms, you had five.

They did things carefully, as Richard explains: 'We investigated the idea of buying up cheap property in the rougher areas of Newcastle by renting out an apartment in Scotswood, but fortunately we hadn't bought the place ourselves. It was a tester to see if buying up cheap property in the worst areas of town, then renting it out, would work. Its failure proved that it's always better to buy in an expensive area rather than a cheap area...'

Geoff Gillie would say that's typical of the way Richard works. 'Richard gets an idea, he puts his toe in the water and tests it out, and very quickly decides whether there's any money to be made – whether he can make a fortune out of it – and, if not, he moves on. If there is, he'll make a massive investment.

'He'll weigh up any business deal, suss it out and ask himself "Can I do this? Do I want to do this? Can I be bothered to do this?" – although he can always be bothered to do something, because he's hyperactive. But that would have been typical of him – he saw a good opportunity in these cheap apartments, had a go at it, found it didn't make enough money, or that the risks outweighed the benefits, so he moved on!'

Their property interests required large sums to be paid out on maintenance, which in turn led to them dabbling in soft furnishings, but there wasn't a good enough return to be had from that. Meanwhile, Richard spent a lot of time going to franchise exhibitions, and considered a number of options including cleaning franchises, but the idea he and Jeremy settled on was franchised plumbing – FastFix, the precursor of HomeServe.

Jeremy: 'We were both still looking for ideas, and I remember we both went to a national franchise exhibition. We saw a business called First Call that we both thought looked like a really great idea – guys in yellow vans, call-out within an hour, 24-hour emergency service in all trades. So to find out more about it and potentially to do it, we talked about becoming a franchisee for them, but, having been through the initial discussions, we decided we could do this ourselves.

'I was still working in consultancy, so Richard initiated the set-up of what became FastFix. He set it up and started running it out of the office that we then had to run the property business. The bottom line was that it was a great idea, with great marketing – Yellow Pages advertising, loads of calls coming in – but we didn't know anything about running a contracting business. We had a lot of cash tied up in it…'

It was certainly a learning experience. One trick Richard quickly learned was that you had to be number one in the Yellow Pages. 'I thought "You can't just put Fastfix, because you'll be halfway down the list", so we became A1 FastFix – a permutation that would always appear first in the Yellow Pages listing. These days you can

The Journal/**Tuesday, August 11, 1992**

Journal

ISSUES THAT MATTER

Fleet's in: Richard Harpin with one of Fastfix's fleet of vans.

One-stop craftsmen's shop

By BUSINESS STAFF

A NEW one-stop property repair and maintenance service for businesses has been launched in the North-East.

The service provided by A1 Fastfix will mean a single phone call will bring either a plumber, electrician, joiner or builder.

Multi-skilled workmen are available with the flexibility to tackle any type of work.

A1 Fastfix is the idea of partners Richard Harpin and Jeremy Middleton, who run the Newcastle-based Professional Properties group.

Their other businesses include property development, letting and management, mortgage advice and interior design.

"One of the biggest problems people experience is getting hold of a workman, particularly in an emergency," said Harpin. "With this service there's someone answering the phone 24 hours a day, 365 days a year.

"We can handle anything from a broken heating system to a complete refurbishment. It's a one-stop shop effectively."

Harpin believes the service could save businesses money. "It means they don't have to keep an in-house maintenance team."

Professional Properties employs 25 people and has a turnover of nearly £500,000 a year. Harpin and Middleton plan to franchise the A1 Fastfix business throughout the country during the next two years.

The service will have a fleet of bright yellow vans, initially covering most of Tyneside, Northumberland and Wearside. It will also be available to private householders.

"The cost of a job will depend upon the degree of urgency," said Harpin. "An emergency is charged at our highest rate, but if you wait a week it's much cheaper.

"We also offer a keyholder service, so we can deal with emergencies without having to call out staff."

look in Yellow Pages and you'll see dozens of different companies using the same trick.'

Unfortunately, as Jeremy recalls, things weren't going according to plan. 'After the first full year – or perhaps the first accounting period – of this, we discovered that I'd made £100,000 [in management consultancy], which was pretty good, but unfortunately FastFix had lost £100,000. So at that stage things didn't look all that great. There was plenty of promise, but it was about then that cash started to get really tight, and it got really tough. We were struggling to pay the wages, and ended up putting them on our credit cards because we simply had no other means of paying them. We'd spent all our tenants' deposits covering losses in the business – I should stress that this was not illegal at the time, but we would have been liable for it. It was later that tenancy legislation was introduced to make it illegal... We would have paid it back somehow, but we had no more cash anywhere.'

Quite simply, the two of them were trying to run too many businesses, and the inevitable happened – they ran out of money. As well as A1 Fastfix they had Professional Properties doing property letting and management, interior design and decorating businesses and a mobile ironing service – they were trying to do too much.

Because of their cash flow issues, they did a deal with the VAT people whereby they wouldn't collect what was due for that quarter, and payment would be deferred until the New Year. Nevertheless, a bailiff was sent round to Jeremy's house around Christmas Eve to take some furniture away...fortunately, he'd never told his wife about any of the problems, so when she answered the door she pleaded ignorance, but Jeremy remains 'deeply unimpressed that they didn't seem to have paid any attention to our situation...'

'But something had to be done,' admits Richard. 'We each took out £10,000 from our credit cards, and I borrowed £10,000 from my mother without my father finding out. My mother's only regret now is that it wasn't ten thousand that went into HomeServe as an equity stake.

'I also had a friend at the time called Simon Blunt, whom I'd only known for two months. Sometimes in life you meet people and know immediately they're going to be a lifelong friend. I think I'm quite a good judge of character, and if I click with somebody you have that lifelong friendship. I'd only known him for a short while, but I invited him to Newcastle for a weekend and gave him such a good time that by the time he got back on the train to Derby on the Sunday afternoon he was absolutely worn out! We'd been hunting in north Northumberland, we'd been out on the town every night, and he'd written me a cheque for £15,000. We did give him a 20% interest rate, so when he says he's the one that really bailed me out I do remind him what he charged in interest!

Simon takes up the story: ' I met Richard at a franchise show at the NEC in Birmingham, and we became friends. He invited me up to Newcastle to meet himself and Jeremy Middleton... Anyway, the next day I was on the train on the way home from Newcastle – I was probably still drunk – I suddenly realised where I was and what I had been doing. I reached inside my suit pocket pulled out my cheque book and the nightmare was there on my cheque stub: £15,000 to Harpin & Middleton!

'We'd been very drunk, obviously, we'd had a very good night, and they'd shown me round all their businesses and offered me a stake in their enterprises or 20% interest, because the loan was unsecured. So I looked at them and said "Guys, the shares aren't worth anything, so I'll take the interest rate" even though it was unsecured and it was quite risky. Obviously, as you can imagine, our mutual friends remind me about this all the time. I think he offered me 10% of the shares in his first ventures – if you take that and look at the HomeServe share price, you can see I'd be worth lots of money now… Instead I earned myself £3,000 interest!

'He paid me back, and about a year later I was getting out of his new Porsche in Hagley Road, in Birmingham, and I said to him, "That money I lent you, I'd put it at 50-50 I'd ever get it back." He snorted and said, "It was more like 99-1 against"!' (Their meeting was at TGI Fridays restaurant, where Richard took a liking to their waitress and offered her a job as call-centre team leader – then walked out having completely forgotten to pay the bill!)

'I remember talking to my cousin Richard Blunt, who used to work for the venture capitalists 3i. He'd met Richard, and I told him at the time about lending £15,000 to him and asked whether he'd have done it, and he said, "That guy's either going to be the next Richard Branson, or he'll end up in prison!" Thankfully it's the former…

'So despite only getting £3,000 interest, whereas potentially I could have had shares in all his ventures including HomeServe, I've greatly benefited from my friendship with Richard, because he's given me lots of good advice over the years in my own business…'

Richard put in a manager to run a Mortgage Advice Shop franchise and ended up selling it on and taking the business idea and developing it with Simon. At one point he had a third ownership of Mortgage Advice Bureau, which was an improved model of Mortgage Advice Shop. Today, that has become a national business and remains successful despite the economic downturn, and is the reason Simon and Richard have remained close friends. Simon recently invited Richard to be godfather to his daughter Jemima.

The last word in this chapter goes to Jeremy: ‘Richard can certainly cope with failure, but he doesn’t accept it. We had plenty of failures, but he just regards them as learning points along the way. He’s always been totally resilient, and always focused on to the next thing that was going to work – he’s never been put off in the slightest, and he’s still not, which is why he does well, really. He always overcomes adversity…’

Chapter 4

It's not the idea, it's making it happen

'I've learned that you can't expand a business and grow it into profit. If you can't make something work on a small scale, all that will happen on a bigger scale is that it will lose more money.'

Richard Harpin left Deloittes in 1991 and set up a management consultancy with Jeremy Middleton called the Marketing Department. 'The first job he got us,' Richard remembers, 'was to advise South Staffs Water in Walsall whether they should set up a plumbing service. I said I'd go and do it. I got employed on a consultancy basis in December 1992. It was a six-week job…and I never left!'

Jeremy, who had been doing quite a bit of work selling to the newly-privatised utilities suggesting they should look at new and related business ideas, takes up the story: 'The strategy was to write to utility companies – and it could have been electricity or water – and say "Why don't you look at going into this sort of business?" – in other words a HomeServe-type operation. The pitch was that we were a very experienced team of management consultants, used to working on utility diversification with experience in this area because we also run a business in it, so why don't we look at it for you?

'We got to the proposal stage with a number of people, but none of them took it any further until we went to see South Staffordshire Water, where we spoke to Steve Coathup, their Finance Director. I got a consultancy contract with South Staffs to look at plumbing – they were planning to do a direct labour, regional operation.

'The conclusion we presented to them was that it was a terrible idea as it stood, but that there was a better one. Going into plumbing was a good idea, since it was part of their brand, but it needed to be national to take advantage of economies of scale, and it needed to be emergency-focused rather than based simply on everyday plumbing jobs. We also recommended that they do it as a franchise operation, and pointed out that, although they were ideally placed to do it, they were a water company with no experience of running this kind of operation. They should have some kind of skilled management team to run it for them, and our recommendation was that they should do it with us.

'The final part of the deal was that we would put in a small test operation called A1 Fastfix which we had set up in Newcastle, they would provide the working capital we needed and the brand name, and we'd split the business 50-50. And broadly, they agreed. They came along and did their due diligence… they sent a chap who spent a day pottering round the office and said everything was fine – I don't know if they realised it was losing £100,000 a year – and away we went.

'I can't remember whether they took over the existing company, or whether we set up a new company and transferred the assets into it – I think it was probably the latter. In principle it was going to be a 50-50 joint venture, but it took nearly two years before the final legal document was signed, so we operated on the basis of a two-page heads of agreement in the meantime.

'Richard transferred down there and was operating out of their head office as FastFix, or FastFix Plumbing & Heating as it was at that stage. I was talking to Steve Coathup for about two years before they finally signed, although from my point of view it wasn't until it was actually signed and sealed that I could relax and look forward to making some money! Richard, of course, was always completely confident that it was going to make our fortunes, and never had any of these doubts.'

This manoeuvre had, at a stroke, sorted out the problem of A1 Fastfix losing money and opened up an exciting new business opportunity with substantial financial backing. When South Staffs put in £100,000 for 52 per cent of a new company, HomeServe, Richard and Jeremy had the remaining 48 per cent between them. The company was set up in April 1993 when the water board agreed the deal. Little did South Staffs realise that in less than a decade the tail would be wagging the dog!

As initially set up, the business generated work through the water company call centre when customers rang up saying they needed a plumber – but it was a model that never really worked. In practice, it simply isn't viable to have a workforce, however small, hanging around all day and being paid in the hope that someone is going to call with a plumbing emergency. From a financial perspective, sub-contract labour is much more attractive than permanent staffing – the company only pays for the work that's done, but the downside is that it can never be sure the labour will be available when the jobs arrive.

Lindsay Bury was chairman of South Staffs at the time Richard and Jeremy got involved. And, as he recalls, they arrived at just the right moment. 'We backed quite a few little businesses, with varying degrees of success, by way of diversification from the water company. This was a bit different. It wasn't an established business, Richard came along with an idea of starting a plumbing franchise, and because plumbing's related to water, we thought "OK…"

'We invested £100,000 in the company, for which we got a 52 per cent share, but we also negotiated an option whereby we could go up in two stages, first to 62.5 per cent and then to 75 on a very low formula – a price/earnings ratio of 4. So that was pretty attractive for us – we would have control, and if it proved successful we could buy up to 75 per cent. John Harris, who's since died but was Chief Executive of South Staffs at the time, was the man who negotiated that deal, and from then on we saw Richard continuously as the thing gradually got going.

'Richard is strangely compelling. He certainly had something about him, and he was an imaginative and determined young man. He was very focused and he knew exactly what he wanted. I suppose we were all a bit sceptical about whether there really was a business there, and initially I personally couldn't see why people would pay simply to have a plumber come round to them… obviously if a flood wrecks your house, that's a different matter, but you're covered on your household comprehensive policy for that. I couldn't quite see why people were in such a state about their plumbing…

'Richard was very impressive, actually… a slim, small guy, but very intense. He knew what he wanted, knew what he was trying to do and he was very persuasive. He used to come into board meetings, and I remember he brought in a pair of pale blue slippers that he was proposing should be issued free to the plumbers so that, when they were clumping around people's houses, they wouldn't dirty the place!' (RH: The plumbers still wear those boot-covers today!)

'The idea of the franchise was a bit of a shambles, actually, and it wasn't very well-run to start with. It wasn't until he brought in an ex-Army guy called Bankie Williams that he began to get a grip on it. Richard isn't great when it comes to detail – by which I mean that, although he's good with detail conceptually, I don't think he's a good operations man; that's not his strength.

'The plumbing franchise was pretty unsuccessful, and at one point we got involved in litigation with some of the plumbers…I've never been very keen on the idea of franchising, and to my mind this was another example of franchising not really working.'

Lindsay was right. The business plan was for HomeServe to break even in Year 1 and be making £1m profit by Year 5 – ambitious, with the benefit of hindsight. However, there were losses of £500,000 in Year 1 and South Staffs were threatening to make a rights issue or even to close the business. Richard needed to persuade the Water Company to continue to back him, as his Newcastle friend Geoff Gillie recalls.

'There was a pivotal moment when Richard and I were playing golf one Sunday morning and Richard said to me "I've got a tough week coming up." I said, "Why? What's going on?" He said, "I've got to try to persuade the main board at South Staffs that they should keep on running with this, because at the moment I just keep on losing money… I know I can make this work, but I just haven't found the right way yet. I've been thinking about it, and I've got to change their opinion of me… I've got to find a new vision so I can keep doing this a bit longer."

'I asked him what the idea was, and he said it was water insurance – that was the way forward. We looked at each other for a few seconds and said "What are you talking about, water insurance, why would you want to insure your water pipes? I mean, you get burst pipes, but that's not the water company's problem, so what's the vision?"

'He explained it to us, but to be honest we just couldn't see it working – and told him it sounded like he'd be kicked out by the end of the week! But, lo and behold, he sold them the idea, and that gave him more time which was really the start of it all – then he really started to make the money.'

South Staffs had been supportive in getting the business up and running, and they didn't actually take the decision to shut it. While half a million in losses was a considerable amount to Richard and Jeremy, Lindsay Bury feels the sum was relatively minor in their scheme of things. 'I can't remember any point at which the board was tempted to walk away. After all, our investment was very small – half a million was all we'd put in, it really wasn't a big deal.'

Jeremy Middleton concurs. 'South Staffs weren't just going to walk away at some point without making a serious investment, which we knew we needed. It's better to have a small piece of a big, successful pie than to have a big piece of something that isn't going anywhere.'

'Even so, the situation was serious and needed rectifying,' admits Richard. 'There was a joke that went round concerning myself and John Harris, a lovely bloke no longer with us, who was the Chief Executive of the water company group at the time. The joke went:

"What's John Harris bought his children for Christmas? A Cowboy outfit…called FastFix!" I saw the funny side, but vowed that one day we'd be bigger than the water company.

'In fairness, South Staffs had been incredibly supportive. They put in the money but it was more than that; they helped me set up a small business. They gave me a table with three legs – the fourth was missing but that didn't matter, it just about stood up. That was the post table on which we opened all the letters with the application forms filled in. They got the telecoms manager to set up a few phones, the IT manager to set up a little software system to run the business. So all the things you'd take for granted as a big business, they put those people to work on setting it up. You can't underestimate the value of that.

'So it was more than the kind of backing you'd expect from a private equity house where they just give you the money – South Staffs gave a little bit of management support, although the management was really me, with Jeremy as a non-executive adviser and part-owner of the business.'

David Sankey was a non-executive director on the board of South Staffordshire Water, and sat as one of the board at the water company that signed off the agreement to launch the business.

'Water-company people tend to be fairly staid and conservative, and Richard, of course, is quite the opposite. He's very dynamic and very active, committed and enthusiastic about everything he does. He believes very strongly in everything he does, and that goes an awfully long way towards making things work.

'One thing about Richard,' he observes, 'is that he never takes no for an answer. Even though you might say to him "Richard, that's a complete load of rubbish...", a few months later he'll come back with exactly the same idea, argue it a bit differently and probably get away with it. He's a very good salesman, whose strength lies in being able to sell the ideas and being determined to get them through, no matter what. No entrepreneur is terribly good at the detail, all entrepreneurs need people to tidy up after them, but Richard is very good at employing the right people to do that.'

There were a few culture clashes to overcome. Because the deal took time to be signed, Richard remained as a consultant for quite a while in the early days before finally joining the payroll. As someone used to getting things done quickly and on his own terms, Richard found some of his dealings with the water company rather irritating. Little things, like signing off expenses and so on, but unsettling nonetheless.

'At the time, there was this thing about cars,' he recalls. 'You couldn't come to work in a sports car because it was a water company. I said "Okay, I understand that you get the standard issue water company van or car... Not a problem," I said, "but allow me to come to work in whatever I want when HomeServe is making more money than South Staffs." That was the deal and they probably thought I was going to bring my second-hand Porsche, not my first helicopter! But let's not get ahead of ourselves...'

A key player in the new operation was Jennifer Synnott. She had been at South Staffs for five or six years and was released to the FastFix operation on Richard's arrival. She stayed until 2009, when she left to take a career break.

'When Richard first recruited me,' she reflects, 'there wasn't a HomeServe as we know it today, it consisted of some temporary staff and a three-legged table, so Richard didn't have much to sell me in terms of a career path. But what he did have to sell was a vision. It's probably the strangest interview I've ever had in my life… He did all of the talking and most of the selling – I think he asked me two questions – but he had such a passionate, clear vision of what he wanted to achieve.

'Obviously the vision he had then wasn't anywhere near where HomeServe is today, but I'd worked at South Staffs Water for a number of years, I was in my early to mid-twenties, I'd done my MBA, and I was keen to get other experience. I suppose it was a little bit of a gamble because there wasn't really anything other than Richard's passion and enthusiasm – it was infectious. I thought, at my age, with no mortgage to pay, it'll be a great experience. I don't think I could possibly have guessed where it would have ended up, and over the years his enthusiasm has increased, if anything, rather than waned. It can be very tiring at times (laughs)...and a little frustrating!

'People have asked my why I stayed at HomeServe for so long, and I think it's mainly because no two days are ever alike – certainly every year is different… There were ambitious growth plans from day one. It just kept growing and growing. 20 per cent year-on-year growth is, in itself, no mean feat, but I think, as the person behind the scenes putting the operation together, trying to develop discipline, control, and a platform that will deliver Richard's vision, it was very challenging. The ideas change quite frequently, as well, and I think that's what maintains your interest, along with his sheer energy and determination.

'Sometimes, when you've run a company for a number of years and it's quite successful, you start becoming, not quite complacent, but perhaps your own energy levels drop… But you only have to watch Richard giving a presentation to the staff, or whoever, and it just ignites you again because he genuinely believes in what he tells you, which is very exciting.

'I think that, initially, South Staffs found Richard's approach quite amusing – he was the guy that turned up in the Porsche on day one, that sort of thing… So Richard adapted his behaviour – he stopped bringing the Porsche to work and switched to a clapped-out Rover for a while. I can remember spending many hours in it tootling up and down the country! But I think they were always exceptionally supportive at senior level, it was a joint venture, and whilst there was a differing mindset there was still a lot of support.

'I think at certain times it brought some good discipline – Richard's entrepreneurial spirit would sometimes lead him to jump very quickly into things and waste money or shoot off in the wrong direction, so I think that having the extra discipline of corporate governance around it perhaps helped HomeServe in the early days.

'In terms of the business from a lower-level perspective, I came from South Staffs and I knew a lot of people, and in the early days that was really helpful because we didn't have any money. So if I wanted a little favour done, say an IT favour or wanting to borrow some desks, I could have a word with the boys in the call centre and they'd help move stuff and so on… You couldn't possibly do that now for health and safety reasons, cost centre reasons, that sort of thing, but in the early days it worked really well.'

As HomeServe started to become more successful, South Staffs could see that the venture was starting to go somewhere, but cultural differences re-emerged. 'We certainly came across some when we were looking for extra space,' Jennifer confirms. 'We moved into one office – and this was how tight space was – where, apart from an entry and an exit, we sealed off the two other doors. But we had to take the doorknobs off the inside just to create the narrowest of walkways so we could get around!

'On a personal level, although I was leaving colleagues behind, I was doing lots of different things as the scope of the role became wider and having an absolutely great time, working really hard and doing long hours, but having a ball doing it.

'But as HomeServe grew, those little favours disappeared. We started off in what might best be described as a pig-pen, a small area surrounded by screens, then we moved into a little office. Then we needed to use significantly more space, so we moved to the first floor, which involved some other people moving out. These were people who'd worked for the water company whose status was defined by the amount of floor space they had – they might have been middle managers but, because they'd been there for 20 years, they'd got three more filing cabinets than someone else…

'These were massively important things to them, and of course it was all down to HomeServe and Richard Harpin, this upstart – who'd long since stopped arriving at work in his Porsche, but these things are remembered – and I think that's when some of these cultural differences started to become apparent. I think it still probably helped that I was ex-South Staffs, so I knew a lot of them anyway… Also, when we started to get that little bit bigger, we started to recruit one or two of them, and I think they began to think "Well, if you can't beat them…" But I think there was always that little bit of friction.'

At this stage, Richard was commuting to Birmingham from Newcastle every week. Despite the pressures of work he was still spending weekends happily socialising with friends, as Geoff Gillie recalls: 'Richard was in the throes of all the trouble with setting up at South Staffs Water, and he was losing money all the time and commuting to and from Birmingham every week, but he still got round to organising a surprise 30th birthday party for me. A little later I did the same for him.

Mr. Richard Harpin

requests the pleasure of the company of

to celebrate his 21st birthday

30th Birthday

on Saturday 10th September 7.00pm for 7.30pm at

Millfield House, Jesmond Dene, Jesmond,

Newcastle upon Tyne.

RSVP

6 Ilford Rd. Jesmond,

Newcastle upon Tyne,

NE2 3NX.

Tel: 091 213 2500

Black Tie *Carriages 1am*

'He got in touch with my mother, and spoke to a couple of the girls we were friendly with at the time, then arranged to get the spare set of house keys that I used to keep at my mother's place at the time. He got the keys to some mutual friends, got the girls to make a whole load of food, then got my brother and some of our friends to put the word out…we had about 60 people in the house. He'd sorted out all the booze, all the food and done all of the invitations. I guess that's pretty typical of Richard – he gets things done, sorts everything out and loves arranging things.'

Richard had bought a flat in Birmingham, and would travel down from Newcastle early each Monday morning and go back on Friday night. He had a flatmate, Rachael Hughes, who was working for GKN at the time and rented a room. This is how Rachael remembers things:

'We were flatmates for most of 1994, just before I went to Latin America. I had just left University and was on a graduate management development programme with the British company GKN. This was based in Redditch and GKN required all its graduate trainees to live in the area. All my fellow trainees wanted to live together in the same conditions they had as University students, which was absolutely abhorrent to me! I didn't want to live on my own, so I looked in the newspapers for a flatshare and that's how I hooked up with Richard.

'I didn't like Birmingham particularly, and he was only there because he had the consultancy job with South Staffordshire Water. He had literally just come up with a business plan about doing plumbing insurance. He thought it was a great idea and managed to convince South Staffs to do a joint venture. Our flatshare worked quite well because he would be off home on a Friday afternoon and so I had the flat to myself for the weekend!

'He was 29 at the time – I remember it was his 30th birthday in September 1994. He felt that he might be on to something with the plumbing insurance, but I think he felt that with every single business venture he did. He'd had several – some that had worked and others that hadn't worked out – and at the time was running a number of other businesses. He was still very much in partnership with Jeremy, who was running their consultancy business. He decided to devote himself full-time to the plumbing thing. They also had Professional Properties, a property letting and management business up in Newcastle, and several other irons in the fire.

'There are some things about Richard that haven't changed at all. He was absolutely determined to make a success of himself, and to become a millionaire by the time he was 30, which I think he managed. I don't know if he managed it in net assets but he certainly managed it in gross!

'He was still very much attached to the material aspects that success could give him, and the effect it had on girls. He'd drive round in his red Porsche and found that it was a great pick-up line. He was very proud of all that and that has never changed. Back at that time of his life he had what he still has now – a child-like need to change everything into a competition, and win it.'

Richard was certainly facing a challenge – the business was losing £10,000 a week. Every week the business grew, but the break-even point moved further and further away. It proved to be another valuable business lesson: 'I learned that you can't expand a business and grow it into profit – either it works or it doesn't. There were worries that we were never going to get to the break-even point – my friends and colleagues were saying "Richard, I know you wanted to run a big business, but you're going to have to think about what proper job you're going to do when this fails…"'

Whilst the water company management had been very supportive and put in £100,000, they suddenly realised that the business had run up half a million in losses in the first year, and there were fears that they might decide to close it down. It was time for a serious rethink, as Richard acknowledges.

'In that context, you think "Well, what am I going to do? Am I going to stick with it, and prove that I can actually come through, and I will find light at the end of the tunnel, or am I going to say that everybody's telling me to give up, so I will and I'll pack my bags and decide that running a business is not for me, so I'll go and work for someone else again…"

'We'd built up a network of plumbers, we were advertising in Yellow Pages, but the economic model didn't work. One of the biggest bits of learning was this: We had this break-even graph and I used to think that if the business is not profitable but you grow it bigger you'll be able to cover your overheads. It doesn't work. If you can't make something work on a small scale, all that will happen on a bigger scale is that it will lose more money.

'So there was this elusive break-even point. Every month sales went up and every month the break-even point was this much away. How were we going to get there? The answer couldn't be by continuing to roll out a model that doesn't work – in these situations you've got to find a model that does work.'

What Richard needed was a solution that produced a positive, predictable cash flow which would enable him to fund the right level of plumbing service to homeowners, while also providing money to finance the development of the business. He couldn't make the economics work by offering a plumbing service based on a price-per-job, so he began to look at a model that, instead, incorporated an annual fee, and thus provided the predictability he needed. The solution, to disguise an insurance policy as a club membership and take the premiums as fees, changed the way he thought as he began to realise how much money the business could potentially make.

Nick Duxbury, a friend of Richard's at University who now lives a few miles from him in Yorkshire, remembers the two of them having a conversation at a party about a lady called Patsy Bloom who founded the Pet Plan Group in the Seventies.

Her dog was sick, with a history of illness, and she hit on the idea of starting a health insurance scheme for animals since she was paying a fortune in vets' fees. She found a business partner and they each invested £250 into the new venture. Sixteen years later, Bloom had created a business with a turnover of £20 million. In 1996, when Pet Plan had 400,000 policy holders and turnover of £40 million, she sold out to Cornhill Insurance (later Allianz) for £32.5 million – a near-65,000-fold return for her and her business partner on their initial joint £500 investment.

That conversation took place in the early days of setting the business up, and Nick says that the fact that they'd had that discussion meant his friend was thinking along the same lines. Richard agrees.

'I was determined that I had to find a way for this to be the Big Idea. I was trying to work out how we could make this business work in a few areas of the UK, not even thinking about a national business. It never even crossed my mind – and it wouldn't have been right at the time anyway – that one day this would prove the model even beyond the UK…

'Every business should write a business plan of sorts, but think twice about a five-year one. Three years is a long time in the history of most businesses particularly the young entrepreneurial startup ones. It's really about the first year, and many business plans will bear no resemblance to what actually happens in reality.

The major bit of learning is do your research but be flexible enough to adapt, do things on a small enough scale to test and learn so you don't throw away all the money until you've found the magic winning formula. And in the first year we hadn't found the winning formula.'

The turning point came when Richard discovered a little water company in the South of England who had got a plumbing insurance programme running. At the time, they had about 28,000 members, impressive for a small water company. So he hired a market research agency to get some of their customers into the local Holiday Inn, and sat in the room listening to what they said. Two of the points raised that day provided the basis for all that followed. 'Why does somebody come out and inspect the underground water pipe in our garden', one customer asked, 'when if something goes wrong and it bursts we can see it 'cos there'll be a fountain in the garden. Why don't they just cover that in case it goes wrong?'

Another said 'I'd also like the plumbing in my house to be covered because I know that's not covered by my insurance unless it causes damage to my ceiling, in which case the consequential damage of the replastering and redecorating will be covered by the household insurance, but not the call-out and the plumbing repair itself.'

Richard spotted the gap in the market: 'So I said "That's a good idea – we'll brand it to the water company and we'll sell it by direct mail..." Lo and behold, light at end of the tunnel. Today that little water company has 35,000 customers signed up and we have over nine million policies. The moral of the story is: it's not the idea, it's making it happen.'

It very nearly didn't happen, but Harpin remains convinced that if you stick at something and you're committed to it, you will make it. He's also a firm believer in learning from parallel markets, and learning from others. 'There's no such thing as a good idea: it's about taking an idea, adapting, evolving, innovating, developing, challenging and testing.

'The insurance plan was the way to make it work. Once we made that work with a thousand leaflets we made it work with a hundred thousand next, and then into millions. That was the model that took the business from half a million pounds loss in year one to three quarters of a million profit in year two.'

Harpin devours business biographies and scribbles in the back of each book summarising the lessons learned. 'One of the books I read once was How To Think Like A Millionaire [by Mark Fisher and Marc Allen]. And there were some very simple messages in there.

> First, if you are really determined and you stick with it you'll make it – whoever you are – if you've got that belief and determination. Second, tell people. Because that embarrasses you into having to do it, and, third, it's then about where you set the bar – whether you want to make a million, ten million, a hundred million…'

Jeremy Middleton's take on what led up to the Eureka!' moment is typically matter-of-fact: 'There are a few different bases, I suppose. The first one was "It's a good idea, let's do it". The second one was "We're not going to succeed, we need the backing of a better brand" – and some cash – and the third, and most important was to turn the model around to the AA-style service. The confirmation comes when researchers and focus groups say "Yes, it's a good idea", and when you do a mailshot you can be sure of the response rate – then you know how much you can spend, and that's when all the marketing logic and the direct mail skills come in. I think HomeServe has a pretty sophisticated direct mail operation… and they're not afraid to spend some money, but that attitude comes from Procter & Gamble as well.'

The initial test of the insurance idea was launched in September 1994 and rolled out on a much larger scale in the following April. In effect, it was born of desperation – how were they going to make the business work? It was quite clear that opening more new Yellow Pages areas and expanding wasn't going to achieve anything – they had to find the model that worked. Richard acknowledges that desperation can be a very creative thing: 'If you convince yourself you're desperate, the model is not working but you're going to stick with it, you'll find a solution.'

Selling the idea again to the South Staffs board was relatively easy because they knew all about Richard's determination by now. His insistence that he wasn't going to let them close the business or call a rights issue left the water company in no doubt of how determined he was to make things work. Fortunately, the initial direct mail campaign had come up trumps – they had a 3.8 per cent take-up after sending out the first thousand leaflets and had people sending in their cheques for £40.

'That was getting our marketing investment back on the members who were going to be with us for several years in the first year,' says Richard, 'and even making money on that. It was just unbelievable.

Conventional wisdom in direct marketing, at least at that time, was to brand the envelope so that the recipients knew what was inside. Instead, these leaflets were made to look official and water company branded, the idea being that householders would hang on to them and read them rather than put them in the recycling.

The initial offer was that, for £40 a year, customers would get £1,000 worth of cover for blocked drains or burst pipes with a guarantee of a two-hour call out and all costs covered. As already mentioned, the initial mail-out achieved a 3.8 per cent take up from those 1,000 leaflets – and, while a figure of 38 households signed up might not sound that impressive, it has to be borne in mind that the industry standard rate is around 1 per cent. The initial results were, then, very encouraging, but the second mail-out, of 100,000 leaflets, achieved an identical 3.8 per cent take-up rate, confirming it had been no fluke.

HomeServe was finally on its way.

Chapter 5

Stick with it and think big

'I think one of the biggest lessons I've learned in business is that there's always light at the end of the tunnel, and far too many people give up, particularly on a new business. They blame recession, which is particularly relevant currently, or they blame somebody else, another business, or the market.'

Richard had run five businesses by the time he was 20, and this, at last, was the 'Big Idea'. While most of the others had been pretty successful, he had always felt that there's a limit to how many businesses you can set up and run, sell on, or move on from before you really have to pin your colours to the mast and say 'This is the one, this is the Big Idea'. He'd finally made that commitment, but the reality was proving difficult.

'I think one of the biggest lessons I've learned in business' he says, 'is that there's always light at the end of the tunnel, and far too many people give up, particularly on a new business. They blame recession, which is particularly relevant currently, or they blame somebody else, another business, or the market.

> 'Trying to write a business plan for a new business is absolutely essential, including doing as much practical research in the market as you can, talking to as many people as possible, mystery shopping, doing all these things means you can really check it out before you put your money and yourself on the line, you've always got to remember that, having done all that and written the plan, that's not going to be the reality. The key thing is how much you want this business to work.'

Richard decided that this was his last opportunity and he had to make it work. He was determined to find that solution and because he was so determined, it became self-fulfilling. When things become difficult, it's essential to test every possibility in the search for a business model that works. In this case, as we've seen, the business model that worked wasn't opening up new areas every month and recruiting sub-contractors to do the work, because the break-even point was getting further and further away every month as the business grew. If the economic model isn't working then getting bigger isn't going to solve the problem. You need to change the model to get to profit.

The magic here was sending out the 1,000 leaflets asking customers to pay the £40 for a year's cover and sign up, and that suddenly turned a business that was losing half a million pounds a year into one that made three-quarters of a million pounds profit overnight. Jeremy Middleton was, of course, still very much involved, and this is how he saw things:

'The business plan showed us going up from X to Y and never losing any money, but what actually happened was that in the first year we lost £500,000. We were waiting for the axe to fall, but South Staffs were very good and continued to support us. In fact, we were still facing a number of difficulties associated with the fact that we still didn't really know how to run a plumbing business very well, and these persisted until the development of the warranty proposition.

'At the time, a very small company in Surrey was offering an underground water pipe policy with an annual inspection that appeared to be quite popular.

'This was the "Eureka!" moment – we both saw that and thought it was a fantastic idea, so we did a spot of very quick research, developed our product which included plumbing and drains and excluded the annual inspection which was costly and not seen as a benefit. We then did some direct mailing, and saw there was a great response, and it's all come from the development of that idea… as soon as we saw that working, it was all a question of marketing drive, marketing development and rolling it out big, and that is what Richard has done.

'All his life, he's been starting up businesses, looking for something that really works, and he often thinks he's found it…on this occasion, he had found it, and that's when the drive kicks in, and the dynamism and the focus. That's when we turned the business around and started to make some serious money.

'In commercial terms, that's the story – I remained as a non-executive director on that business all the way through, so I've seen it closely, but it's been Richard running it. We were 50-50 partners originally, but there was a bonus provision brought in at one point – we were each entitled to ten per cent of the profits – and at one stage I saw him completely working flat out in Walsall, having moved away, and I was doing other things, so I said "Okay, I'll take over our shared consulting business and you can have the bonus provision." Now ten per cent, pre-tax, became a very generous proposition, which South Staffs bought him out of later on with some more equity…so we worked that one out amongst ourselves.'

So from the point where the company was £500,000 in debt, and it looked like South Staffs might close the operation, they'd turned things round. What was the secret? In three words, 'stick with it'. Then it was about two words rolling out the business: 'think big!'

'Once we'd proven out that 1,000 leaflet mail-out and got our magic 3.8 per cent take-up,' Richard explains, 'we mailed out 100,000, then we mailed out a million, and today we're mailing about 60 million marketing packs a year. Our marketing spend last year was around £50 million and there will be a big increase in investment across our three marketing divisions – UK, Europe and the US – over the next 12 months… So, once you've proved something out, think big, but don't think big until you've proved it out, otherwise you risk blowing everything on one idea.'

But, he warns, 'Most ideas are not successful – fortunately we've had a pretty good run in terms of ideas that we've proven out, but there are plenty that don't work, so it's down to making sure that you test on a small scale until the idea is proven out, and if you then need to re-test it on a larger scale, do so before you roll it out on a massive scale… but you'll never take over the world unless you think big.'

The first-year loss of £500,000 was transformed into £750,000 profit in the second year. Today HomeServe is one of the UK's largest direct mailers, sending over 75 million items through the post each year – and this success was built on an initial foundation of a 1,000-piece mailing! That certainly flies in the face of the direct marketing 'rule' that at least 35,000 pieces are needed to be able to test a mail-shot objectively (at the 95 per cent confidence interval).

After the first successful marketing shot with South Staffs, approaches were made to the other UK water companies and, within a short time, they had full UK coverage, including Scottish Water. Jennifer Synnott was very much involved in the expansion programme.

'The next hurdle to get over was expanding it,' she explains, 'because we weren't a household brand, we were just a West Midlands company with a small customer base if we continued just to do this out of South Staffs. At that point we weren't even HomeServe, we were Home Service Scheme… It was about taking this idea out to water companies and putting together a deal that took the risk away from them. I think we were fortunate in that this was around the time of the privatisation of the water companies, and South Staffs was already privately owned, so I think they were a little more forward-thinking than Severn Trent and the other big ones.

'So, privatisation took place, and the water companies were desperately looking for other sources of income, but they weren't necessarily set up for it. Richard and I went out a bit like good cop/bad cop, although in our case it was more like "sales cop/service cop", and he would knock on door after door after door, and eventually we'd get a meeting arranged. Richard would concentrate on the sales stuff, highlighting how we'd take all the risks and do the marketing and service etc., and the water company would have a guaranteed income stream – then I'd tell them how we were going to do it.

'These people were risk-averse, worried about their reputation because we wanted to use their name. They were also very concerned about OFWAT and levels of service. They were under considerable pressure within their business to cut costs and still deliver – a lot of them simply weren't set up to do it – so it was about offering something, but also saying to them "Don't worry, this guy might be a bit scary, ex-Procter & Gamble, a marketeer – a very different animal to you – but I'm the same animal as you, and I'm the one who's going to do it." We just needed them to agree, then we could get it up and running. We mirrored their service levels, and away we went…

'The more partners we got, the more people could see how successful it was, and the easier it became to get other partners. At this stage, we were still linked in to South Staffs – we already had companies like Thames and Anglian on-board before we separated the HomeServe business from South Staffs.'

But Home Service Scheme didn't stop at plumbing. As they already had access to a large customer base it was a simple step to offer other home emergency services as well, and these had a high take-up rate. The operating model for the business was that the 'membership' fee gets paid by the customer whether or not a cost is incurred in getting 'the man in the van' to fix anything. The club membership fee is the insurance premium, a proportion of which is paid away to the underwriter for taking the risk that a cost – the cost of repair – is going to be incurred.

As chairman of South Staffs Water, Lindsay Bury had bought into the original proposition. Now things had been turned around he was more than enthusiastic about Richard's next initiative.

'Richard had another inspired idea, that we should go into affinity marketing – which meant not selling [plumbing insurance] under our name but branded also to the other water companies. Clearly, if it worked for South Staffordshire Water, there was no reason why it shouldn't work for all the other water companies. The first company Richard went to was Anglian Water, and they agreed to be the guinea-pig for the new approach. They started marketing an "Anglian" policy, so customers thought they were dealing with Anglian – but they weren't, they were dealing with us.

'All the contracts were HomeServe contracts, and we really only paid Anglian an agency fee, basically to cover the use of their name. Money for nothing, really, but it was attractive to them because it used their name... of course, first they had to be satisfied that the service was a good one, but they must have been because they went ahead and lent their name to it and gradually began to sell quite a lot of these policies.

'To make it work, we had to set up a call centre and invest quite a bit, but the economics of selling an annual policy were good, even after paying Anglian Water a commission and paying the underwriters for taking the risk.

'It soon turned out to be good business for the underwriters, because there wasn't a great deal of risk involved. We did toy with the idea of taking the risk ourselves, but in the end we didn't because we weren't in the insurance business and we thought that if the worst happened and everybody's pipes burst, we'd have a flood of claims, and that would end up distorting our own profitability.

'So when this was such a success with Anglian, who are one of the ten major water companies, we gradually picked off the whole country. We had Thames, Severn Trent, Southern, Northumbrian, Yorkshire…one or two of them resisted and said they'd do it themselves, but that didn't last long because they didn't do it as well as we did, got fed up with it and came back to us.

'Once we'd sold the idea to most of the major water companies, we quickly built up to a substantial number of policies, and we had a very good cashflow. It was an extraordinary achievement… It's an absolutely brilliant business, and it all stemmed from the seed idea of the plumbing business.

As the business grew, Richard strengthened the operation by bringing in a lot of new people, and they soon had their own building adjacent to South Staffordshire's headquarters in Walsall. Jennifer Synnott remembers the establishment of HomeServe's own building in 2001 as one of the really significant points in the company's history. Not least because, while office space may have been a minor consideration to Richard, conditions for his staff were becoming cramped.

'We'd go to one of the water companies,' she recollects, 'and we'd end up with a new affinity partner – and, once that was done, Richard was on to the next thing. Following behind was poor old me, trying to put the infrastructure in place with very little cash – and certainly the issue of how we were going to support each venture was never part of the decision-making process. Quite often we were having to persuade South Staffs to knock down some walls to make our space a bit bigger…

'So the new building was not only needed but significant. It was purpose-built, on the South Staffs site, and I'll never forget Richard, myself and [former South Staffs chief executive] Brian Whitty walking around this building. I think Brian was getting the jitters because we had this huge great open space, and we'd only got around 50 staff at the time, all shoved in a tiny little area… Brian was saying, "What if we don't fill it?" and Richard was saying, "Of course we're going to fill it! We're going to fill it in two years…" We filled it in a year, and we were on to the next thing.

'That was pretty much a key moment for me…and I think it helped to make you feel that you were part of something that was real and tangible, rather than being stuck in this guinea-pig enclosure that was shunted around.

Moving to the other building the one that superseded the one on the South Staffs site in 2001 was also notable, but I think the next big moment was in 1999 when we got our millionth customer. We emptied the building and got all the staff out into the car park for a big celebration. We all stood in the car park drinking champagne – which was really bizarre on the South Staffs site, where they didn't allow drinking, although it was only a glass each.

'It was "Everybody stop – you're all doing a great job and this is a monumental moment for us", and we all stood there with Richard doing his little speech, and I thought "Yeah, this is kind of special..."'

On the personal front, Richard enjoyed another special moment in July 1997 when he and Kate married – it's a date Richard is guaranteed never to forget, since he has it engraved on his cufflinks! The couple began married life in Nottingham, which at least meant that commuting to Walsall was less demanding than it had been from Newcastle.

Would the advent of marriage mean Richard Harpin might not be running quite as fast? No, but twinkling feet would soon be augmented by whirling rotor blades…

Chapter 6

Find an opportunity in every problem

'There are a lot of rules in life- people can choose to ignore them, and let life carry them along at its own speed and direction, but the people who create a lot of value and wealth are those that create their own template and follow it.'

The HomeServe transformation was well under way. By Year 5, the business was making £7 million a year compared to the original target of £1 million. But since the dash for this impressive level of growth was led from the front, pressures on Richard's time grew even faster. So he took a leaf out of Lord Hanson's book and learned to fly in 1998. Since then, the helicopter has been a key tool in helping him to make best use of his time, and, since relocating his domestic base to Yorkshire, taking him home to his family at the end of the working day.

It hasn't all been clear skies for HomeServe, though. 'We've had a few moments where the business could have closed down,' says Richard, 'because water companies were taking over responsibility for providing a free repair service for underground water pipes. Deputy Prime Minister John Prescott in the 1999 Water Summit summoned all the water company chiefs and told them they needed to repair all their underground pipes because there was too much leakage. We thought "What are we going to do, because this is an integral part of our product?"

'It was the big picture of the magic fountain coming out of somebody's lawn from the very beginning of this business, so the whole business could have been threatened. It's important to find an opportunity in every problem, and we saw the biggest period of growth in the history of HomeServe coming out of the gloom of possibly having to withdraw that cover from all of our policies.'

In the end the water companies only offered a limited free service and HomeServe then developed 'Gold Standard' cover, offering a two-hour response, up to £2,000 to cover an underground pipe repair or replacement and cover for reinstatement works. Under this arrangement, the basic service the water companies provided was that they would come out in five days, rather than two hours, repair only a small section of the water pipe, and simply fill in the hole afterwards, but they wouldn't re-surface the drive or replace any lost planting. The HomeServe policy included all of those things, and represented excellent value at less than £20 per year. No surprise, then, that HomeServe have since sold more than two million Supply Pipe Cover policies.

'It was a problem at the time,' Richard admits, 'thinking how we were going to avert disaster, but we turned it into a big opportunity. It gave us our fastest period of growth- – but it was only by battling away and thinking "There's got to be an opportunity here…"' But growth can bring its own problems and challenges. As long-time employee Jennifer Synnott recalls, HomeServe's history has seen growth spurts followed by periods of consolidation.

'Looking back, it seemed that about every three years we'd have one of these periods of consolidation, during which we'd also be planning growth – but you won't see that in the numbers. We still had that 20%-plus growth, but about every three years the business had a step-change so it was that much larger.

'From an operational perspective, it was about looking at costs, because for a few years you'd be throwing money at it to keep up with the rate of growth, then you'd get to the stage where you'd be haemorrhaging money and you'd have to consolidate. That didn't stop the marketeers, and the ideas men, they'd still keep going, so you'd still see that overall growth, but there were periods of consolidation. And as the business has got larger, those consolidation periods have got tougher…

'If you look at the business, it's still very seasonal, and the vast majority of our activity, and our income, happen at the back end of the year, which causes operational problems... It's just the nature of the products – if you're worried about a burst pipe or whatever, it's a winter thing, and although we have pest policies to protect against rats, mice and wasps, in general they're cross-sell policies (ie sold to existing members), so the acquisitional policies, the ones that customers buy into HomeServe for, are typically quite seasonal.

'Broadly, marketing takes place between September and March, so if you spend too much of your marketing budget in the summer, you can end up with problems if your take-up rate is low. So there is a dip, and each year it's bigger. We've got some warranty products now that help to fill the gap, so that trough isn't quite so pronounced in the summer period, but it's still there, and even the warranties are slightly seasonal – people will often buy a new washing machine or cooker in the run-up to Christmas.'

By 2003, HomeServe had become bigger than South Staffs and Richard decided it was time to separate the business from its water company parent. 'It was becoming difficult to get great people into the business,' he explains, 'marketeers, service people and so on, and it took a couple of goes to persuade everyone it was for the best. We managed to do so about a year after we started down that track. We thought through all the ways we could split HomeServe and the best was to put the water company back into the water sector, because we'd moved into support services on the back of HomeServe.'

The water company was demerged and listed in its own right and the continuing company was renamed HomeServe. Richard's shareholding, and Jeremy Middleton's, had to be reversed out of the original HomeServe subsidiary so they had shares in the listed company.

Jeremy saw the sense in demerging: ' The business just grew so fast, and we were generating more profit than South Staffs. We simply got bigger than them, and we had all the growth potential – and when we looked at the value of the business, we were worth more than they were.

'It made sense to have the balance of power shifted, and it also made sense for the shareholders if the businesses were separated because they were so different. So the existing plc was renamed HomeServe, and we basically sold off the water company – in fact it was demerged as a listed company, and the shareholders who remained with it did very well when it was sold off. I kept my shares and did quite well when it was sold on to someone else…'

As Brian Whitty recalls, this happy state of affairs had hardly been anticipated. 'When I joined (South Staffs) there was a five-year plan in place and it said that the water company was going to make something like £15 million profit by the year 2000 and Home Service (as it was then known) was going to make a million. (Consultants) Arthur Andersen reviewed this plan and said the water company profits looked sensible but the Home Service forecast was hugely optimistic – it was never going to happen. The water company profits came within £50,000 – turnover and cost was about 2 million out each but the final result was within £50,000. And I think that year Home Service made about seven million pounds. No way we could have anticipated this huge success, which was beyond even Richard's wildest dreams.'

Jennifer Synnott recalls the demerger as another of those special moments. 'About a year before, we had a two-day management conference with about eight of us who were the directors of the business at the time. We mocked-up a newspaper clipping that said that in such-and-such a year HomeServe would float on the Stock Market as a FTSE250 company, we'd have an office in New York, and had various other "facts and figures". It was all a complete fantasy, but what we were trying to do was to articulate, in one easy-to-read piece, where we wanted to be as a director/management team. We looked at it and thought "That's all very nice" and we shared it with some of the senior managers in the business at the time – we still weren't very big. But then, when South Staffs Water was demerged leaving a standalone HomeServe I remember picking it up and looking at it with some of the new people in the business.

'Funnily enough, it wasn't Richard who came up with that idea, it was Jonathan King, the MD of the UK business at the time. But we spent two days kicking around what our vision meant to us, and I think all the Directors at the time had a slightly different take on it.

Lots of questions to consider… I think it was a way of sitting down together and saying "Okay, some of the detailed stuff needs to be worked out, but let's at least agree and work collectively to get the bigger picture down on paper – what does it look like, how is it going to feel, how many people are we going to have and what's that going to mean?" So each of us had something to take from the article, and we could see how our area would look when we got to this point…. it was an absolute stroke of genius, although it didn't feel like it at the time when we were all sitting there late into the night…

'In the end, it was a really good motivational tool. Sometimes, when you bring new people into the business, it's hard for them to realise just how far we've come in such a short period of time, so quite often they'll highlight the fact that the IT systems aren't quite what they should be or whatever. But this wasn't a multi-million pound set-up operation, it was built up from nothing, so we had to earn the money before we could spend it. Looking at that mocked-up newspaper clipping, which had been dated to say when we'd written it and when we thought it all might happen, I'd say that around 80% of it had a very close correlation with what actually happened, which was really fascinating.

'I thought that not only was this business going places, it was going places because we were making it do so, and we were making it go where we wanted. It was no accident. Some of the critics have said that HomeServe has been lucky, found a niche in the market and so on, but no, we know what we're doing, we know where we're going, and we know how to get there…that realisation was very exciting.'

Lindsay Bury, who had been chairman of South Staffs for a great many years, took the opportunity to bow out and pursue other interests. 'HomeServe began to assume considerable importance in the South Staffs accounts because it was contributing a lot of the company's profits. Then Richard no longer wanted to be a subsidiary of South Staffs, and we, meanwhile, had gone on to own 75 per cent of the HomeServe business through exercising the two options I described earlier.

'At that point we obviously had control, but we thought it was in the interests of South Staffs and shareholders that we split the company and give the shareholders some shares in South Staffs, and some in HomeServe. Richard was then independent while Brian Whitty, who was the chief executive (of South Staffs), became the chairman of HomeServe.

'What happened to the share prices after that was remarkable. When we split the company, if I remember correctly, South Staffs shares stood at about 640p, having steadily risen over a long period because of the success of HomeServe... So when we split, South Staffs shares were about 640p, as were HomeServe's. Within eighteen months, South Staffs shares had gone above £11.00 and they were taken over by a private equity group, and since then the company has been sold again at even greater value, so it was very good for the water company. HomeServe shares rose from 640p to a high of, I think, over £20.00... so it was a real bonanza for the shareholders of both companies.

'Richard's an endlessly creative marketeer, and since hitting on the Big Idea of the insurance policies he's bought a few companies – while HomeServe was still with South Staffs he bought Regency, a company that was offering extended warranties on things like three piece suites, and the guy that was running it in Weston-Super-Mare was making quite a lot of money out of it. We paid £40million for it – too much, it wasn't worth that much, but the idea was where

Richard wanted to go. We then bought another business in Norwich that did glazing repairs, locks and so on... these weren't initially successful ventures, but I think he's stuck with them and added to them and improved them, and in many respects they were only bad buys because he paid over the odds for them.

'Conceptually, Richard knows where he wants to be... he's made some acquisitions that were overpriced, or he's bought them perhaps a bit early – as people do – but I think he's learned from that, and these days he's pretty well where he wants to be with his strategic vision.'

The red van that is now HomeServe's trademark was fast becoming a familiar sight across the country. It was another example of the Harpin approach to marketing and branding, as Richard explains. 'I wanted a van that stood out from "white van man", which is really our competition – the self-employed local contractor, driving a white van, working from home. They have difficulty doing emergency work because they're out on another job; you get their answerphone or they're out of reception on the mobile so they can't get out there in two hours like we can.

'I wanted something distinctive, and, at the time, I thought about us as the fifth Emergency Service...the AA are the fourth, and we're really the AA of home emergencies. So I thought we'd have a van that's bright. I remember when the firemen came into my son's playgroup; I saw the fire engine, bright red, and I thought "That's the colour for HomeServe!" That's the reason I painted my helicopter red, with the HomeServe logo, as well...'

HomeServe was now standing happily on its own two feet. There was some concern initially that Richard might sell a large proportion of his shareholding, but things settled down after he made it clear that he was prepared to commit to not selling, and in fact on three

subsequent occasions he has borrowed to buy more shares at £8, £14 and even a few at £18. 'It's such a great business,' he insists, 'and still undervalued, so I could use the shares I had as security to buy more. We're talking ten or twelve million pounds, a lot of money.

> I don't know many other people who would have gone out and borrowed that amount to invest in stock. It's called putting your money where your mouth is – something I've always been happy to do.

'Hopefully people who know me wouldn't say I have an inflated ego. I'm down-to-earth, a hard worker that gets out of bed at five o'clock in the morning. One of the things Jeremy Middleton said at my 40th birthday party was that I should occasionally look back and think about my successes. But my nature is always to look forward, to look for the next thing to achieve.

> 'Why am I so driven? What I think I've got is determination beyond anyone else, and a vision of providing a service that's currently missing from most households around the world.

While there will be sacrifices in me taking HomeServe worldwide, I want to be able to see as much of my wife and children as possible. I try to make sure I can, by using the helicopter, getting home for before bedtime occasionally – probably less than I claim, as my wife Kate keeps reminding me – but if you've got something that's a half-good idea and you know you can make it happen, you've proved it in a few countries, then I think you owe it to homeowners, and to the team, to stick with it and make it happen. That's the reason I get out of bed!

'You occasionally worry about it all going wrong. All my wealth is in HomeServe on paper, and occasionally I worry about making sure it doesn't all disappear. I think every entrepreneur has those worries – I don't worry about it too often because it's "so far so good", but there's a long way to go and I'm going to stick with it until the time that there are better people to run the business than me. But I'm having a great time, and all the while I'm adding value to the business there's nothing I enjoy more than running HomeServe. Eventually, I've got many more things I'm going to do – but right now, I haven't even got time to think about them.'

Perhaps surprisingly, Richard Harpin's success in business does not extend to investing in other companies on a personal basis. 'I've dabbled in investing in shares over the years,' he admits, 'but I've probably never made any money on them other than HomeServe shares because I've tended to go for high growth stocks and the ones that did well were offset by the ones that did badly. I've always read Analyst magazine, which later became Outstanding Companies Digest, and I only ever made money out of companies that it featured, which formed the basis for my investment decisions in buying other shares… I always thought it would be good, if I were running a company, to have it end up being featured as one of the top companies in Analyst magazine.

I wrote to them suggesting that they feature HomeServe, but didn't hear anything from them, and then suddenly, one day, it happened. Editor Jeremy Utton has kindly supplied us with his analysis of the business for this book.

'My relationship with Richard goes back maybe six years, as an investment analyst. We first looked at HomeServe when I was working as an investment analyst. My background as an investment analyst goes back around 30 years, to the late Seventies. During the Eighties and Nineties, in search of a credible philosophy, I started reading all the books on the great investors, as some analysts do – although many don't – and I became familiar with Phil Fisher, the great American investor, and Benjamin Graham, who is the founder of the whole discipline of Security Analysis.

'Warren Buffet, now the wealthiest man in the world, is a disciple of Graham's. In the late Eighties and early Nineties, Buffet wasn't really recognised over here, and was really barely recognised in the States. In the late Nineties, I started importing investment books from the States as part of my investment analysis business, and around that time a lot of guys in the States started writing books about Buffet. The more I learned about Warren Buffet, the more I realised that his style was at odds with the way most people try to invest, and the way they try to identify successful businesses.

Instead of having a very short-term view on market prices, Buffet took a long-term view of the quality of companies and businesses and overlaid all his investment decisions with a specific set of criteria that businesses had to match. These were very objective, rather than the subjective views that people generally have on stocks. You might hear people say "The market's up", or "The market's down", 'This is cheap', 'This is expensive' and so on – all very subjective stuff – and there was really no template that you could build a strategy on.

'The long and the short of it was that Buffet was the best player in the game, he had an identifiable strategy, and if you took the time to look at what he did, you could then, in basic terms, imitate the sorts of things that he was doing. In around 1996 or 1997, two people in the States, Mary Buffet, who was Warren's daughter-in-law, and David Clark produced a book called Buffetology, which was the first definitive, mathematical handle on what Warren Buffet did. That was a major forward step in a number of people's thinking about what defined a quality business, and we started to use the criteria that Buffet sets out in our analytical work.

'Now, at the same time, Richard was developing HomeServe, initially within another public company, and then on its own, and the kind of characteristics that are apparent in the HomeServe business are exactly the kind of characteristics that we'd seen when trying to define the ideal business template, the sort of business that made a good long-term investment.

These were the things that came together in my head. Obviously there are other listed businesses around that fit similar criteria – they grow, they earn high returns on the capital invested in the business, they have a predictable model, they're relatively simple, straightforward businesses, they generate high incremental returns on capital and generate a lot of free cash flow. There are characteristics that the great businesses match, and the companies that Buffet has bought in the past, and continues to buy today – American Express, McDonald's, Coca-Cola, Wells Fargo and so on – almost all match the same criteria.

'With HomeServe you have a predictable, successful, value-generating business and that, coupled with Richard's dynamism and personality, is what has made HomeServe such a success. When you look at the most successful businesses over the last ten years or so, a lot of them have very similar 'shapes' in terms of the way they're structured. These characteristics are the things that generate exceptional value for owners – and with Richard being the largest owner in HomeServe, it's allowed him to capture an awful lot of value! A lot of it is down to the way he's modelled the company, as well as his dynamism, personality and foresight.

'There are a lot of rules in life – people can choose to ignore them, and let life carry them along at its own speed and direction, but the people who create a lot of value and wealth are those that create their own template and follow it. It may owe something to their own personality, and the specific template may work better for them than for anyone else, but in all cases it will be something that generates value and wealth.

'Another thing is that people are great starters in life, but not great finishers – Richard has been very single-minded and focused, and he's stuck to things that work for him, things that he can see will produce a lot of predictable long-term value. A lot of people go off the track – they're great at starting something, but then they get sidetracked into doing something else, or something comes on to their desk that diffuses their focus… Richard is a very focused individual.

'Warren Buffet always says that you're better to have a modest sailor behind the wheel of a speedboat than you are to have an accomplished sea captain in a rowing boat. So, if you're an average guy in a very good business model, you'll do better than a very good guy stuck in a lousy business model, but what you've got with Richard and HomeServe is the best of both. You've got a very shrewd guy, and a very personable guy with a lot of drive, determination and foresight overseeing what is a very good wealth-creating model – you've got a double-whammy there, really...

'He's doing fine in France, and he's beginning to rack up some policies in the States as well. It's early days in the States... usually things work in reverse, and it's Elvis Presley or McDonald's that starts over there and becomes popular over here, but it doesn't often work the other way. From the way Richard goes at things, there's no reason to suppose that he's not going to be successful in the States. They've got the same customer-focused structures, and they have the same requirement for these affinity-backed policies and services that Richard's so good at, so I don't see any particular reason why it shouldn't work there. You do need very good on-the-spot management, though, because it's a long way across the Atlantic. It's easy to start something in Walsall and sort things out in a small country like the UK, but with an American operation, unless you have good managers that you can have total trust in, that distance can create a lot of uncertainty. You can't see what's happening, so you need to have people you can trust and who understand your philosophy.

'I think the key thing to wealth generation is getting the model – the template – right, because a lot of businesses, both those listed on the Stock Market and private businesses, will go round this rat-wheel of activity. It's like putting alcohol through a still – you pour it in the top, and it goes through all these tubes and processes on the way down through the still, and when you turn the tap at the bottom, not a lot comes out. Exactly the same can happen with cash going though a business.

'At the end of the day, a business is only a device to generate cash for its owners. Looking at it very simply, an investment is all about laying cash out today in the hope or expectation that you're going to get a lot more cash out of that investment further down the road. Investments in businesses have to return cash to the owners or entrepreneurs at some point in order to be regarded as successful, because you can't spend factories and you can't spend stock…the only thing the owner can spend is cash, and once cash becomes distributable all cash spends the same. Some business models are very good at generating cash for their owners, others are bad, and the majority of businesses are frankly average. Now, what you've got with HomeServe is a very good device, or mechanism, for generating net distributable cash, and that's the way real economic value is generated.

'One of the great skills that Richard shares with Warren Buffet is being able to eliminate those things that you don't need to focus on. It's the personality type, and the discipline working together on an economic model that's capable of generating predictable value over time.'

Chapter 7

Get the right people into the business

'You need to stay focussed – you need to keep asking 'Where do we add value? What are our Crown Jewels? What are we really good at, and which bits do we do better than anyone else?'

Picking the right people and paying them an appropriate rate for the job has been a crucial factor in HomeServe's success story. Richard's philosophy on incentives and rewards is typically straightforward.

'By paying the best you get the best, and this makes a huge difference to the long-term future of the business. By and large, HomeServe keeps its good people. The loyal and the smart get promoted and rewarded beyond their dreams. Those that haven't got what it takes move on. Those who fit simply don't want to leave. Why would they? Key people are well incentivised. Share-based incentives have proved easier to put in place since the de-merger with South Staffs. Staff are rewarded through executive share incentive schemes, LTIPs, key executive incentive plans, annual bonuses and a sharesave programme. And, at the coal face, the key incentive among operators is the Fitter Package – the more 'right first time' jobs the engineers do, the more they get paid.'

HomeServe GB has been a Sunday Times Best Employer for five years: they aim to make it a good place to work and people are well rewarded if they make the grade. Jennifer Synnott describes potential HomeServe employees as 'maverick spirits', and goes on to say:

'Richard is entrepreneurial, and even though the business has changed dramatically, and his approach has tempered somewhat, he's still an entrepreneur at heart. Yes, he does genuinely believe in the people in the business, and he believes that great people make the business what it is, but he also believes in finding new people who will help to take it to the next level as well, so it can be a bit like hanging on to the coat-tails and seeing how far you can go with it…

'For senior appointments, Richard has had, for a number of years, what amounts to a personal headhunter to help fill posts where he feels he needs a "serious hitter"… That's been very much his approach, looking out for great people all the time.

'A common factor in these people is that they're highly motivated, but they have to share Richard's passion and vision as well. They also have to be able to work with a disciplined approach that's suited to the company the size it is today, and come up with lots of ideas, but also have an entrepreneurial edge. He'll perhaps look for somebody who's very corporate, very blue-chip – not quite with the character that they enjoy that kind of environment, perhaps with a little uncertainty about what's actually happening next. I think somebody that's used to a bureaucratic type of environment doesn't stay long…

'Richard is still quite ruthless because he remains true to his vision and his goals, 110%, so, unless you're adding value, or he perceives that you're adding value – which I suppose is the important thing! – he can be quite ruthless. While I've worked with Richard for 15 years, other people haven't stayed that long – and some have been invited to leave over the years because it's just not been for them.'

'I think what Richard realised early on, and still realises now, is that in order for him to be successful, and for the business to be successful, it is about getting the right people into the business. That's always been Richard's mantra. He's a strong marketeer himself, that's his interest, but if he can get other strong marketeers in to get things done quicker or better, or enhance them, then he'll do that as well…'

Richard regards having good people, the right people, as essential, because whether you're going to employ 50 people, 500 people, or the 5,500 people that HomeServe employs today, you need to get the right balance. His natural style is to lead by example, and he's more than happy to roll up his sleeves and get involved, but he also appreciates the value of being able to trust others to get things done. He believes it's essential to be able to attract great people into the business, and then give them the autonomy to make their own mistakes while growing the business. And one of the best ways of doing that is to hire people at a more junior level, get them into the business and then promote the right person later on.

'I've certainly been very successful in finding people myself,' he says, 'I'm a firm believer in doing so – and some of the best people we've brought into the business have been those I've come across myself and said "One day I'll have a job for that person". One of the best examples is Jonathan King, whom I met at a friend's 40th birthday party in Nottingham, and I thought "He's a smart guy." He was running Boot's Healthcare International and previously he'd been the Brand Manager for Boot's No.7, and I thought "I can't afford him now, I haven't got a job for him, but I reckon I will have." Within six months I'd persuaded him to join us as business development director in the UK membership business.

Within a year, Jonathan had risen to become MD of UK membership, and about three and a half years ago Richard persuaded him to go over to the US, where the business had been growing very slowly and urgent action needed to be taken to speed up growth. Jonathan justified Richard's faith in him by going from the biggest part of the HomeServe business to the smallest, achieving a massive turnaround and leading the US operation into profit for the first time, which has paid huge dividends. 'He's been successful,' Richard asserts, 'because he's brought great experience and learning from elsewhere and he's a high-calibre individual. But he'd also grown with the business, and he knew the HomeServe culture, and he'd done it in the UK, so I knew he'd replicate that in the US.

Richard's former flatmate Rachael Hughes is another example of bringing in the right person for the job. Having rented a room in Richard's flat in Birmingham, Rachael moved on, working for GKN in Leatherhead and, at one point, actually renting a room from Richard's brother, Stephen. After that, Richard lost contact with her because she went abroad to set up a GKN joint venture, and later set up businesses in Chile and Argentina, but when he was considering who to get on board to help set up HomeServe's French operation, Rachael, a fluent French-speaker, came to mind.

'I tracked her down to Buenos Aires,' he recalls, 'flew her into Miami, and persuaded her that day… I had to hire a big motorboat, and a helicopter to fly around the Miami skyline – over Gloria

Estefan's house with me at the controls – but eventually, before she got on the flight back to Buenos Aires that evening, she'd agreed to my offer.'

Rachael started in France with three people, in what HomeServe regarded as a 'torture test'. The feeling was that if they could pull it off in the most difficult European country, they could make it work anywhere. It almost didn't work: 'We listened to the French, and they said "Your model won't work in our country – it needs to be more complicated, dual branded…" We spent a year there, and we failed.'

Just when they were on the verge of admitting defeat, they went back to the original cartoon-style mail-outs and proved the original HomeServe model could work in France. A failing take-up rate of half a per cent was transformed into one of almost two per cent overnight, and the French operation has been a tremendous success ever since. Today, HomeServe has sold over one and a half million policies in France, employs 350 people selling a number of the company's products, and has a growth rate of over 30 per cent a year that contributes a significant amount to HomeServe's profits.

'Rachael came and did a tremendous job in France,' acknowledges Richard, 'and then I promoted her to run Europe, which meant getting Spain set up. Now she's starting to acquire businesses to speed up the model, which is how we set things up in both Spain and Belgium.'

A higher-risk method, which is starting to pay enormous dividends at HomeServe, is to hire great people, at a very senior level, externally. The best example is Jon Florsheim, former chief marketing officer at Sky TV. Florsheim had been hugely successful at Sky, taking them from two million customers to eight million, but after lengthy discussions Richard persuaded him to join

HomeServe early in 2007, and he's now doing a great job managing the growth of the UK membership business.

'I've worked for some interesting bosses. I know Alan Sugar reasonably well and Sam Chisholm, whom I worked for at Sky, is pretty aggressive. But there's no aggression in Richard – he may get quietly frustrated but I've never seen him bang the table, ever. A company like Sky is driven by fairly dictatorial people that drove grown men to tears at times. Richard doesn't work like that; he's relentless in his ability to get his idea across. And he does listen.

'HomeServe's a fantastic model and a fantastic story driven by Richard's drive and energy – he's not like an everyday person, but very focused. He's described as an entrepreneur but to me an entrepreneur is someone who flits around from thing to thing, always doing something bigger and better. Richard's stuck to his guns – he's got HomeServe printed through him like a stick of rock. He's absolutely determined to keep on growing the business, bringing in the right people. He's very good but he hasn't got all the answers, so he brings in people who can expand his ideas and take the company to the next stage.'

Richard sums the approach up: 'So... hire great people, but try and do as much as you can on the Procter & Gamble hiring mentality, which is to promote people from within. That's the best way to maintain your culture, and it's also the most motivating for people that are within the business. If they know that all the top jobs are filled by people recruited externally they have a glass ceiling to their career and it's not very motivational. A bit of self-criticism – I think we've gone too much towards hiring externally, and I'd like to go back to doing as much as we can to develop and promote people from within.'

A good example of this is current chief financial officer Martin Bennett, who was promoted from finance director of the UK membership business. Another good example of Richard's firm belief in finding the right people himself came after HomeServe bought Highway Glass, now known as HomeServe Glazing. After the acquisition, the business went from making £3 million profit to breakeven in just 12 months, and attempts to expand the operation just made matters worse.

Quite simply, HomeServe had no experience of running a directly employed man-in-a-van business, and Richard quickly realised that he didn't have the skills to go in and put things right himself. However, HomeServe chairman Brian Whitty was adamant that Richard had bought the business, and so he should go full-time to Norwich, where it was based, and fix it. It was one of the few occasions on which the two men have had a significant difference of opinion.

Sticking to his guns, Richard decided to find someone who could turn the glazing business around. He takes up the story:

'I said "No, I'm going to hire somebody who knows how to run that sort of business," and did some desk research to find someone who had experience of running a directly-employed national business working for insurers.

'I found Ian Carlisle – he was chief executive of our Emergency Repair business until recently – running Autoglass. I looked at several businesses, but Autoglass was the one that stood out, growing its profits consistently, and it looked like a quality customer service operation. So I kept calling Ian until I finally got through to him. I said "You don't know me, but we need to meet up – I've got a potential job for you." He was reluctant, but I persuaded him to join, and he was instrumental in taking our failing glazing business not just back to the £3 million it was making before we bought it, but up to nearly £10 million at one point.'

But as HomeServe continued to grow, Richard found himself with less time to spend doing his own headhunting, and so he took the logical, if unusual step of hiring his own headhunter.

'When I got too busy to do my own headhunting, I headhunted a headhunter! Joel Barnett joined the payroll and was with us for about two-and-a-half years. Initially I said to him "Come and join us for a year, and then you can set up your own business," but he stayed for two-and-a-half years and then set up his own business, still working for us, but on a contract basis rather than fully-employed.

'Many headhunters are good, many of them find people based on an old-boys network, but when I said to Joel if he'd identified five potential people for a job, how many of them would he be able to contact and get in front of me to interview, he looked at me with a strange expression on his face and said: "Well, all five, of course..." Anyone else would probably have said "It depends on whether I can get past the secretary, or who I knew that knew them", and so on. It's all about selling, and every successful person, in whatever job they're doing, has an element of selling – so Joel was fantastic, I hired him, and he's now running a successful business in his own right hopefully off the back of what he did with HomeServe...'

Another important part of the HomeServe philosophy is having a happy workforce. HomeServe GB achieved five consecutive appearances in the Sunday Times' annual list of the 'Top 100 Companies To Work For', an award based on a number of criteria including employee satisfaction surveys. Richard is well aware that happy staff are more productive, and believes there are other, less immediately obvious benefits.

'HomeServe isn't a household name,' he explains, 'so if you're trying to recruit at a senior level, particularly being based in Walsall, you want people either to commute or relocate. There are some nice areas around here, but if you've never heard of the company it might not be an especially attractive proposition. That's when things like being in the Top 100, and the various awards we've won – we won Best Outbound Call Centre in the National Sales Awards, and we've had Best Agent, Best Manager and so on – are as important, because not only do they give our staff kudos but they help with recruitment. Whether it's getting column inches in Marketing Week, or making the Times Top 100 Companies to Work For, it helps quite a lot. When we decide to re-enter it will be in the big companies category with over 5,000 employees.

'Being acclaimed as one of the best companies to work for is not down to luck. I think we recognise the people within our business, and we've always believed in celebrating success, whether that's company success or individual success, like the millionth customer.

'We celebrate any milestone that the business reaches, and we're keen to involve the staff in that, whether it's a free lunch or extra days holiday… we recognise individual performance, as well, so everybody has a basic salary and the opportunity to earn a bonus, but there's extra things we do around that.'

When interviewing for a senior post, getting the right person for the job has always been the overriding factor at HomeServe. If the right candidate comes at £10,000 more than had originally been budgeted for the post, that's not an issue – having the right person will pay dividends later. But, as Jennifer Synnott cautions, everything needs to be done at the right speed.

'Perhaps my biggest challenge over the years has been to say "Hang on, maybe we need to slow down on recruitment here, because we haven't quite got the infrastructure in place yet". Richard would get very frustrated if you spoke like that, he'd say "No, we want to grow this business…"'

And, alongside getting the best people, the key to growing the business is focus. Richard is acutely aware of what HomeServe does well, and determined to concentrate on doing it better than anyone else.

'We could have been distracted,' he reflects, 'by getting into motor insurance, vehicle breakdown, credit card protection – you-name-it insurance – we could have been in it, but what has been really important is having a single-minded vision and concentrating on offering our membership insurance for anything in the home that can go wrong that's not covered by their household insurance policy. That vision developed pretty early on, as soon as we said "Well, actually, can we do anything other than just plumbing and drainage insurance?" And, today, we offer electric, gas and oil central heating, appliance repairs, pest control, etc.

'The only time we've taken a blind alley was in going to do repairs for household insurers, because it's low margin, a very difficult market. We haven't managed to persuade insurers to take on our 'hub proposition', a complete claims handing and repair service. And there are others doing it who are prepared to work for tiny margins, so even extending ourselves in that way, which was very close to our original model, was a mistake.

'You need to stay focussed – you need to keep asking "Where do we add value? What are our Crown Jewels? What are we really good at, and which bits do we do better than anyone else?" – and it's a magical combination of direct marketing of an annual membership for home assistance with providing a repair network that's high-quality, and not doing any more than that. Stay single-minded – everyone that knocks on your door will be trying to persuade you that you should be expanding the breadth of your business in the direction they want to take it – you have to stay true to your core vision.'

Staying true to your core vision doesn't mean you can't adapt and develop it, as Richard explains. 'Chris Zook wrote a book called *Beyond the Core: Expand Your Market Without Abandoning Your Roots* and he said that you're only going to be successful if you expand one bit beyond your core at a time. So, for example, do we want to do repairs for people who don't have a policy? We used to say, "No, get lost, unless you've got a policy, it's tough luck." Now we say, "Yes, we'll do it, at a fixed price, a fair rate, and we'll link in a policy for plumbing and drainage (or whatever kind of job we have just done for them) for the next twelve months", and suddenly we've got a whole new group of younger, less insurance-minded customers. It broadens our market and gives us a new way of getting to them which says "Try the service, you don't have to be a member, you'll be delighted when you have used the service, and we'll sign you up for the next twelve months" – and hopefully for ever…'

Single-mindedness means everybody at HomeServe has a 'To Do' list… But Richard is a big advocate of also having a 'Not To Do' list, on which he keeps all the things that HomeServe are not going to do, the low-priority things that the company simply shouldn't be sidetracked into.

He's learned that as an organisation grows, it generates a whole industry dedicated to doing things that are not relevant to growing the business, so every now and then – and the current recession is a good time to do it – he makes sure the business is back focused on the really important stuff. It's essential to take away the red tape, take away the industry of paper-shuffling, take some unnecessary cost out and get people really focused on growing the product range, improving service delivery, and concentrating on the core. Part of that focus is on making sure that what looks good on paper will work in practice.

'Test, test, test – I can't say it enough… Always test things. Look at normal product launches – 8 out of 10 product launches fail. I think about 60 or 70 percent of our product launches work, but you've got to test things small-scale. Test many ideas but don't test too many variants of the same idea – concentrate on the Big Idea, and put all your effort into that one test. Don't try to test 20 different things in a matrix because it spends too much money and dilutes management attention across too many test legs, so get everything that you think is going to work into those one or two tests and push for the things that are really difficult.

'There are only three or four things a year that make a big difference to a business – make sure you work on those things and push them as hard as possible. Most people give up, and the product launch is not what it could have been, or the Big Idea is thrown away because people are not prepared to knock walls down and jump over barriers to get to the end vision of that new product that's really going to work. The hard bit is battling to get to the really exciting product at the end of it. Don't launch something at half-cock because it's easy, battle for the harder stuff, because that will make the biggest difference…

'I can give you a negative example, currently, which is Landlords' Cover… a great opportunity, very close to our core business, nobody's really doing it – we've only ever done homeowners' cover

– and it's a natural extension, particularly in the current climate, of buy-to-let. We've launched it on the Web, we've launched it in our call centre, we've done a bit of direct mail, but the really hard bit is how we get it built in to the offer that a managing agent, or a household insurer that's offering buy-to-let cover for landlords makes – how do we build it into their proposition? We haven't done that yet, and that's because we gave up halfway, we only did the easy bits, so let's keep battling to get the bit that will sell us 100,000 new policies a year, compared to the eight or ten thousand a year we'll get if we say 'We've done landlords, let's move on to the next thing'. So that would be an example of one where we haven't cracked it, and we've got to push the team to do the hard bit, not just the easy bit.'

One thing that resides permanently on Richard's 'To Do' list is his work on encouraging and promoting apprenticeships. As a member of the national committee of the Apprenticeship Ambassadors Network, he is a strong advocate of apprenticeships, and believes that many more school-leavers should be encouraged to take them up in order to counter the UK's 'skills gap'. Only ten years ago, there were just 60,000 vacancies nationally for apprentices. The work of the Apprentices' Ambassadors Network, of which Richard has been a member for the last eighteen months or so, saw the total rise to 190,000 in 2008, and the aim is to get the number of apprentice vacancies created each year up over 200,000, even in the current recession, a target which they appear to be on track to achieve.

While most of HomeServe's work is currently carried out by subcontractors, Richard is determined that increasing numbers of their tradesmen will be directly employed and franchised in future. As a company, HomeServe is committed to the concept of apprenticeships, and currently have 480 apprentices amongst their

5,500 UK staff, working in their call centre operations and their glazing business. There are more developments in the pipeline – the implementation of a formal accredited apprentice programme for the company's mobile upholsterers is imminent, and there are plans to introduce a plumbing and drainage apprenticeship, not just for HomeServe's own directly-employed plumbers but also for their franchisees and premier contractors to make sure they're bringing apprentices into their own businesses.

It's a project close to Richard's heart. 'I feel passionately – personally, not just within HomeServe – that we need more apprentices. Going back to the fireman analogy of the red HomeServe van, I would like one of our engineers to go and visit every secondary school to do a talk to 11- and 12-year-olds to tell them they don't have to go to university, they could actually do a formal apprenticeship in anything from hotel and catering, to retail, to learning a trade like plumbing, upholstering or fenestration – which is glazing, lock, window and doorframe repairs... I think as a country, we're too willing to send our school-leavers into university education, or computer science, at the expense of getting people into practical work. And certainly, up until very recently and the recession, there was a massive skills shortage in the building industry.

'My only worry is that the current Government have introduced the Schools, Learning & Apprentice Bill, which includes a lot of checks and red tape, and they're also threatening the whole area of Academies. I'm also a great supporter of Academy Schools – philanthropists like Lord Harris of Peckham, the founder of Carpet Right who was the 2007 winner of the UK Entrepreneur Of The Year award, put a lot of time and money into founding Academies.

'Sir Peter Vardy has done the same in the Northeast and I have a brother-in-law, David Dawes, who works in one of the Peter Vardy Academies as a deputy head. Results show that, in the 36 Academies that had two years or more of exam results, even in very poor areas that most of these Academies are in, they massively outperform the schools they superseded, or most other schools in the area. It's all about giving autonomy to the headmaster and to that school, but it's now being jeopardised by this new bill which says that the Government are going to come in and perform some checks, but actually they don't need to. So the Apprentice Bill is good, but not if it jeopardises the Academies.'

Richard wants to take the Apprentice programme and promote it, not just in the UK, but internationally, and he's hoping to achieve this by using the connections he made in Monte Carlo at the 2009 World Final of Entrepreneur Of The Year, enlisting the help of some of the Entrepreneur Of The Year winners from other countries. And preaching this gospel, so to speak, is one of the key reasons for agreeing to the book you're now reading.

'I'm mentor to a managerial networking organisation called the Key Club that is being set up by a woman called Nicola Hain. One of Nicola's ideas was to suggest putting together a teachers' manual to accompany the book you are now reading. The idea has now developed into "Let's bring this to life by taking a version of *Dragon's Den*, a version of *The Apprentice* and this book." So you read a chapter of the book in class or at home, we have teachers' resource material online that brings it to life, and the class is split into two and goes off to do a Lord Sugar-style apprentice challenge, applying some of the lessons learned from the book on their day out doing the challenge. You could have those who actually want to think about a business idea writing a business plan, doing their own research and then bringing it back to a *Dragon's Den*-style panel.

'Richard has offered a free copy of this book to all 3,000 secondary schools in England and Wales together with the accompanying learning materials. There's also a *Charlie & The Chocolate Factory*-style Golden Ticket. If you're one of the lucky five schools that get a Golden Ticket, he will come down to your school, land in the helicopter on your playing field and give you the HomeServe story in person...'

Chapter 8

Speed is undervalued

'Taking too long to do things or make decisions can lose a lot of competitive advantage.'

Richard Harpin's international ambitions are, he admits, particularly ironic given that he speaks no other language than English. 'I once had the misfortune of saying two words in French, at a meeting in France, which were 'cinq plombiers' – five plumbers – and got a big cheer and a laugh from around the table. But other than speaking to taxi drivers and hotel receptionists, I rarely speak any foreign language. It's odd to think that a Brit that was single-language, and not at all multi-cultural, could get a business working internationally and stick with it…one day it'll be worldwide.'

His first attempt to gain a foothold overseas was when HomeServe did a deal with South Staffordshire's principal shareholders, French utility company Compagnie Générale des Eaux, at the start of the

2000s. Unfortunately they had to surrender 60 per cent of the equity and, as a result, HomeServe needed a strong personality to fight their corner. Enter Rachael Hughes.

We have already heard the lengths to which Harpin went to secure the services of his former flatmate. In fact, as she reveals, 'He tried to get me to come back to the UK even earlier, probably 1998… I remember we had to do everything by writing, because he didn't have email. Richard's always been behind with technology!

'He'd wanted me to be MD of what was then Home Hotline in Preston, but I didn't want to come back to the UK. I said that if he decided to develop the business in Europe I'd be interested, and he came back and said that he did. What he had in me was someone who knew how to create businesses and could speak French and Spanish, someone that he knew.'

Hughes had left the UK and, after a short stint in the US, ended up in Mexico as part of the launch team of Chep, a joint pallet-renting venture between GKN and Australian company Brambles. 'That's when I began getting involved in creating businesses. After that I went and did the market development for Chep in South America, so I worked in Argentina and Brazil.

'When Richard first got back in touch, he thought I was still the very financial person I'd been when we first met, but I was far more interested in starting businesses. What persuaded me to come was his ambition to launch beyond the UK, to expand on to the continent. I think he realised that, as the business was doing really well in the UK, it could do well somewhere else. I came back because it was an opportunity to create something and share in the value it would generate. There was a big element of "Come back, start this up and share in the success we're going to have…"'

Harpin had meanwhile persuaded Compagnie Générale des Eaux that they should do a deal in France, 'and they were only prepared to do a deal as a joint venture rather than the usual five year or ten year branding agreement.' It had not been an easy sell, however.

In order to persuade them to do the deal, he had approached Suez-Lyonnaise, their major competitor, and this backfired in what could have been a costly way. 'We showed Suez the model, and then, when we signed with Générale des Eaux, or Veolia as they're now called, Suez copied the model.'

In another piece of bad luck, the first campaign launched five days after the 9/11 atrocity in New York – the mailing had already gone out by the time 9/11 happened. The first policy was sold on 26 September, but response was poor at less than one per cent.

'France didn't work in the first year,' Harpin confirms, 'and we nearly packed it in. Then, out of desperation, we went back to the original UK model, with a cartoon leaflet with water pouring out of the lawn, and that was what worked.' The unsuccessful first model had involved dual branding and an all-encompassing home assistance product rather than just covering the supply pipe. The complicated, high-quality marketing leaflet offered a product that was too expensive, when what was wanted was underground pipe cover, branded as a Générale des Eaux service, for a more modest annual fee of 49 Euros a year.

The mistake had been listening to our French partner,' explains Harpin. 'They said, "Your model won't work in our country – it needs to be more complicated, dual branded…" Just when we were on the point of saying "Well we thought we'd be an international business but we'll just concentrate on getting bigger in the UK", we went back to those original cartoon leaflets and proved the model in France.'

Fortunately, competitors Suez had copied the wrong model. Instead of putting £1 million into the marketing, as had HomeServe/ Générale des Eaux, they'd invested over £5 million. They had no room for manoeuvre and, when it didn't work, decided eventually to shut down the business.

HomeServe's second mailing in May and June 2002 had worked spectacularly, turning a failing take-up rate of 0.5 per cent into nearly 2 per cent overnight, and France has been a tremendous success for HomeServe ever since. In 2009, Richard Harpin could look back on 'one and a half million policies, 350 staff, a national network in France with customers having a choice of three or four of our products, growing at 30 per cent a year and making a significant profit.'

The difficulties Rachael Hughes encountered setting up a business from scratch in France were, she admits, greater than setting up a business from scratch in South America. 'I never imagined French bureaucracy could be so entrenched and so all-pervasive! Administratively, it's just hard work to get anything off the ground in France. I have nothing but admiration for anyone who succeeds there! I had previously set up and run joint-venture businesses, so I knew what it was like to work with two sets of shareholders of different nationalities – but at least the British and the Australians shared much the same language…

'Part of the hard work with this venture was juggling the interests of two sets of shareholders who are culturally poles apart… Our French shareholder is a million miles from Richard, and they needed some more convincing in order to get them to throw their weight behind the project. I've spent a lot of time in this job with one arm stretched forward as I try to hold Richard back a little bit, and one arm stretched backwards as I try to pull the other shareholders forwards.

'But we found a meeting of minds – and, once that common territory was found, Générale des Eaux threw themselves behind the project. Though they're still culturally miles apart today, we've got a very positive French shareholder and we've got a great business here.

'One of the things we needed to do was to focus on following our business model and not to try to please everybody else, including the political interests of the utility. The lesson we've learned is that 80 per cent of the business can be pretty well identical, while the other 20 per cent is local adaptation.

The first year was really tough – really, really tough. We did too much stuff by committee, had too many people participating in the marketing and we lost the focus too easily – so we learned a lesson.'

Once HomeServe had proved that the model could work in France, it was then considered applicable in any other country across the world.

'We've learned an awful lot through doing it in France,' says Hughes. 'We learned a lot about the marketing, about the relationship with utility partners, and about the need to control the network and the service delivery both in terms of cost and quality. Initially we started out not managing our own claims, but eventually, after about four years, we brought that in-house and now, in new countries, we make sure we acquire that capability first in order to give us that base. So it's been a phenomenal way to prove that the model works.

'There are a lot of examples of British businesses that have failed in France. The market looks to what we've done with the French operation to use as the base of its model of what the business could be worth internationally. It's quite a high-profile component of the HomeServe business now and it's taught us a lot. I'm really proud of what we've achieved.'

Hughes sees the future in France as 'a continuing process of developing maturity without losing the focus and the inspiration. To continue to succeed, the business needs to maintain its entrepreneurial qualities, not just in my area of operations but across the board. More and more, I'm bringing in people with real entrepreneurial skills, and one of the challenges for the future of this business is to get the right balance when rewarding these people.

'If you bring people in to start up a business, they're taking a risk. It could all go wrong, and they're leaving secure positions to come over and start something from scratch. They may throw themselves behind things with great entrepreneurial skills, so we need to know how to reward that. That is one of the biggest challenges facing the business.

> 'If you want great entrepreneurs, you have to reward them. It's going to be one of my biggest "people challenges", and I believe the success of the business will depend on our ability to meet it.'

Hughes wants Harpin to continue employing people with talent to make sure that what he establishes gets developed and kept in view. 'Richard wouldn't have made it work in the US by himself – his style just wouldn't have been right – and he wouldn't have made it work in Europe, either. Richard himself could only make it work in England. He set up that business and developed it and ran it – he set up that model – but he couldn't have gone to France and done it himself.

'What you need to achieve that is not an employee who understands the model, but someone with entrepreneurial skills suited to the country. Like Jonathan King, who joined around a year before me. He was involved in the development of the European business, then went back to the UK briefly before heading over to the States.'

King now heads HomeServe's American arm and, as recounted in the previous chapter, was headhunted by Richard Harpin at a birthday party. He took Home Service USA, as the branch of the business is known, into profit in the space of four years after his appointment.

Harpin and King lived close to each other on a private estate in Nottingham called The Park, built in Victorian times for the people who owned the lace mills so they could be close to work but still in the shadow of Nottingham Castle. King takes up the story.

'I was working for Boots, a massive employer in Nottingham, and Richard was commuting to Walsall. Our mutual friend Sara invited us to her 40th birthday party at a restaurant in Nottingham called Hart's. I started talking to this chap who was telling me about his business. I think he described it at the time as being a bit like "the AA for your home", which made the whole thing easy to understand. Then he started telling me about the aeroplane he'd just bought, and I thought to myself "You're obviously doing quite well then, aren't you?"

'This would have been about February or March of 2000...a little bit later, Richard called me and asked me if I'd be interested in talking about a job. We called each other several times, and in the end I decided it was right for me to go and work there. I worked for a big, safe company, a household name, but was getting a bit bored and probably a bit lazy. I was 39, about to hit 40, and I thought I'd like to do something different that would energise me again.'

At the time they met, King was working in international business development at Boots, opening stores in Tokyo – taking a British company and expanding its business model overseas. Harpin could see that he could do the same for HomeServe.

What attracted King to the business was its strong business model. 'It had a powerful competitive advantage because Richard had done deals with the utilities that were long, and exclusive, and therefore protected the business from competition. They were also deals that gave the business access to some very powerful brands – in return for some commission, of course, but in a way that served both parties well. It was also obviously a real customer need that no-one was actually fulfilling, and outside the world of high-tech these things are incredibly rare.

'It's extraordinary, really, that it's something so obvious and simple… even now, and certainly in those days when it was so much smaller, when you tell people about the business, everybody says "What a great idea!" – and really there's nothing that clever about it. It's plumbers, electricians and gas engineers being offered to customers in the same way as roadside assistance is offered by the AA and the RAC, on the basis of a monthly subscription or fee, rather than pay-on-use. A super-simple idea, but no-one had done it…

'The other beauty of the business, and again this is extremely rare these days, is that it had the opportunity to sell things to customers who were buying them for the first time. In most other markets these days, you're trying to persuade someone to buy your version of a product or service rather than somebody else's, but with this, for the vast majority of the customers, we were saying "Here's something you've never heard of before! It'll make your life simpler, why not try it?" It was a universal customer need that was unfulfilled, supported by long-term exclusive branding arrangements. It was a robust business model, and it was already making money… a great idea with very little competition.'

Harpin invited King along to meet the rest of his team, which is something that not many employers would dare to do. 'I got to sit and talk privately to people who were working for him already. One of the things that worried me about moving from a big company to a small company was whether the people who worked with him were good – it's always a good idea to try to work with people who are smarter than you are, because that drives you and keeps you challenged. I was worried that people working for a small company might be doing so because they weren't very good…

'Boots had lots of smart people – arguably too many, because they all just wanted to be in charge of everything – but what I found at Home Service, as it was called then, was that Richard had already gathered round him a group of extremely smart people. They were motivated, they were smart, they understood the business, and that was attractive to me as well.'

King was impressed by the state of urgency that existed at HomeServe. Whereas at Boots, the standard unit of time (the standard response to a request for information) was a week, the standard unit of time at Home Service when he joined as business development director was 30 minutes to an hour. 'There was the expectation that you'd simply do things now. That was enormously refreshing, exactly what I was looking for.

'Speed is undervalued,' he continued, 'taking too long to do things or make decisions can lose a lot of competitive advantage. At Boots, the attitude was that a year to get from an 85 per cent good decision to a 99 per cent good decision was a year well spent, whereas at Home Service the philosophy was that they would take the 85 per cent good decision, try it, and if it didn't work they'd only lost a couple of months. They could go back and change things to make it right and they'd still be better off... '

An affinity for speed was no bad thing, because the challenge King faced when he was sent out to the States was that the business was progressing too slowly. 'If you set the bar at a certain height for yourself,' he says, 'that's as high as you're ever going to jump. What we've had to do here is set the bar higher and acknowledge the enormous opportunity there is in this market. American consumers, just like British ones in the old days when Home Service was young, are, generally speaking, not familiar with the services, and are not being offered them by anyone else. When you say to them "What do you think about this?", most people say it's a fantastic idea and wonder why they didn't think of it...

'There's an enormous opportunity here, and the big challenge hasn't been persuading the consumers to buy what they're offered, the big challenge has been to persuade the utilities here that it's a good idea. We brought over this utility-based model, and the interesting thing about the United States is that the utility market is, in many ways, still less competitive, and therefore less entrepreneurial and less open to new ideas than it is in Britain.'

It was the privatisation background in the UK, and the fact that water companies, having emerged blinking from public ownership, were looking for additional sources of revenue that stimulated a lot of what HomeServe achieved. Whereas in England water supply is 100 per cent private, 80 per cent of water in the US is still supplied by a Government entity rather than a privatised business and electric utilities are by and large still Government or state-mandated regional monopolies.

'But we've made progress,' King states, 'and I've got a bigger team of people out knocking on doors at the utilities here than we ever had in the UK because it's a bigger country, six times the size. There are many different utility companies...something like 70,000 different water systems in the United States, and a surprising number of people who still get their water from a well! There's an enormous number of small towns and communities that have their own water systems they run themselves. We'd have to do deals with all these small utility companies... That's the challenge.'

America is where HomeServe's greatest potential for growth lies, King believes, though he pays tribute to Rachael Hughes' pioneering work in Europe. 'Arguably she's exploited the French opportunity more effectively so far than we've managed in the US...to my great shame! She's got about a million and a half policies, and so far I've only got around 600,000, so she's done incredibly well in a smaller market. But we have potential – it's a bigger country, with six times the population of the UK. In the UK we have something like seven million policies, so that's 14 times the size that we are in the US at the moment, and I think it'd be embarrassing if we couldn't make the US business at least the same size as the UK business.'

The aim in 2009 is to get to at least five million policies within the next five years. 'I appreciate that that's ten times growth in that period, but that's the scale of ambition that we have. I don't think that would be the end of it – I think people would say that's a creditable performance, but at the same time they'd be thinking "Is that all, in a country six times the size of the UK? Is that all you managed to do?"'

Being a Brit in the United States can be a double-edged sword, and King makes a point of not coming over as too 'British'. 'If you're in investment banking, or doing most of your business out of Manhattan, I'd say that being British is definitely not a disadvantage – but if you're trying to sell your services to a utility company in Pittsburgh, or Cleveland, or somewhere like that, it doesn't always go down so well.

'Richard and I have sometimes looked at each other after meetings and said "Well, that went okay, but we came across as terribly British"... Sometimes there'll be another Brit there, and so you've got three of us selling to this dyed-in-the-wool utility executive from Cleveland. What you have to do is imagine it the other way round. You're sitting in Walsall or Burnley, and three smooth-talking Yanks come in and sit in front of you and tell you about this brilliant company they've got... You'd look at them and think, "Do you really know what it's like in Burnley, can you possibly imagine who our customers are?" So we always have to be careful.'

Building a more American team has been another challenge King has faced, though it's of necessity been a gradual process. 'We have some departments where there are no British people at all, and that's good, because we're becoming more of an American company. People appreciate Richard coming over because they know how senior he is, they know he's a successful guy, but ideally we would always mix Richard in with some of our local senior managers – "We're an American business that happens to be owned by a British company."'

In 2007 Home Service USA signed a marketing agreement with FirstEnergy Solutions providing access to an additional 1.1m US households. They also announced the signing of a three-year marketing agreement with Progress Energy Inc to market policies for water-heater repair and replacement to its 2.6 million electricity customer households. And the growth continues.

What do the Americans make of HomeServe and Richard Harpin? 'They admire successful individuals,' King offers, 'probably more than the British. People find his presence very motivating and stimulating. He always comes up with good ideas and he's very good at partnering, getting the business new partners, because people are always very flattered that the founder of the company has come to talk to them. He's a very effective salesperson as well…'

Harpin will be hoping for more occasions like March 2008 when, in the midst of gloomy predictions for the US economy last year and the onset of a worldwide recession, Home Service USA signed a deal with a water company in Kentucky. Louisville, previously best known for hosting golf's Ryder Cup, had a water company with only 250,000 customers, making it an ideal test bed.

HomeServe usually sent its marketing to half the customers – those who are older and who live in older properties with gardens, thinking they were more likely to take out cover. This time, rather than target the market as normal, they decided to send to everybody. The leaflet looked very similar to that initial mailing in the UK, albeit a little more professionally designed and finished. Richard takes up the story…

'The US economy's in the worst recession in history and we're sending out a mailing, branded as Louisville Water, saying pay 60 dollars a year for underground water pipe cover…and 11 per cent of the quarter of a million customers signed up in the first mailing! It was unbelievable. That was one of those "jump up in the air" moments, like when I'd sold a big advertising deal to one of those national clients on Connect magazine, or when we'd got that 3.8 per cent take up (for the first UK HomeServe mailing) when everyone else was doom and gloom – I knew this was going to work.'

There have, however, been occasional setbacks as HomeServe rolled out its model across the globe. An attempt to gain a foothold in Australia was made in 2002, after the French launch but before they set up the US. 'We pulled out,' Harpin recalls, 'because we didn't sell many policies, and in the mailing tests the take-up rates were very low, about a quarter of one per cent. I think Aussies are quite laid back – "If it happens, it happens, and I'll sort it out when it happens" – so they're not insurance-minded...'

There were also problems with plumbers' unions, who claimed that HomeServe were a British company making deals with the local water companies and making Australian plumbers redundant… 'The reality was that we were using them to do the work, but that wasn't the story they wanted to convey. They took the protectionist line…'

The controversy was even talked about in Parliament on a few occasions, Harpin recalls. 'We signed one small Australian water company, South West Water in Adelaide, but there was very little likelihood of us signing bigger companies like the Sydney Water Company because they didn't want the bad press that was coming from the plumbers' unions… We also got a very high claims frequency from the people who did actually join... That was a function of drought areas, and big trees boring their way into drainage pipes to find water.

'So a combination of all those things made us give up on Australia after a year. There were no write-offs because we'd covered the set-ups, it was pretty low cost, and we moved the guy who was MD of that operation into our US operation.'

The year 2009 saw HomeServe acquire a French extended warranty business with 55 staff based in Aix-en-Provence, which was intended to be the beginning of a pan-European extended warranty operation. 'The model now is to use acquisitions to get into a new country,' Harpin explains, quoting Louis Gerstener's assertion that 'the only credible acquisition strategy is an acceleration of your organic growth strategy.'

'I remembered that and, recently, that's guided our acquisitions... Go and buy a sub-contract repair business or a bunch of home assistance policies because these are the businesses we know, and are integral to putting our model together. Then use that as a platform for local management, credibility, buying into some existing profit and a national network to be able to put our business model into.' Interestingly, Harpin claims never to have bought a business that has been for sale.

'No good business is ever on the market and we never buy in competition with others. We persuade people to sell.'

This acquisition model worked well in Spain when HomeServe bought Reparalia for about 25 million Euros in 2007. The strategy is to roll out the red van branding, but with a name that means 'HomeServe' in the local language. 'With Reparalia, we changed our name, HomeServe Iberica, to Reparalia, which is a good Spanish name that means more there than HomeServe… So if you're on holiday in Spain you might see a red van and say "Oh, that looks like a HomeServe van – it's red, it's got the same house logo, but it's called Reparalia."'

The strategy was also used in buying SPT in Belgium, and it's a model HomeServe plan to use to get into Germany, Italy and the rest of the world. 'It repeated the model that was successful in Spain, which was to find a good quality business, with a good management team, to buy, and in Belgium that was SPT, which is run by a guy called Stefan Tournoy. We paid five million Euros for it in December 2008, and he's now integrating that small business into our model and hiring additional management so we can put in the membership model and start signing up a few Belgian utilities. We'll also be looking to extend that business into the Netherlands.'

Next will come Italy and Germany, where HomeServe have identified the businesses they want. 'It's just a matter of persuading the owners to sell at a price that we think is right. I'm convinced that we need to do it by "buy and build" because then we get there quicker.' After that will come Canada, but this operation will initially be run from the US, 'although they're too busy in the US right now to put any resources into opening up Canada. The whole of the team needs to be working on more deals in the US, but Canada will come in due course.'

Richard Harpin believes no markets are unreachable – with a little help. 'You can get in through any door – if it's a steel door with bars you can still get through it if you're determined enough. But it's not just about what you know, it's a bit about who you know. And, having got through the door, if you can have a bit of an introduction, someone who can put in a good word for you it always helps.

'I've used that on a few occasions. In every country we go to now we have introducers help us get in through doors more quickly at a more senior level to help make deals happen for an English business they've never heard of that needs a bit of local credibility and introduction.'

HomeServe's global aspirations have risen considerably in the ten years since Richard and the then general manager of the UK membership business had travelled to Barcelona in an attempt to sign up Agbar, the largest Spanish water company.

'The meeting was in a very old library room with books all the way up to a high ceiling, library ladders and very old-fashioned green velvet drapes. There were about 16 people sitting round the table, all but one of them were smoking, and none of them, bar one, could speak English. Neither my colleague nor I could speak any Spanish, and we were there to present to them the proposition of why they should sign a deal with us so we could open up in Spain…'

After that false start HomeServe recruited capable, multilingual people who, with the assistance of acquisitions, have taken the brand across national borders and put the red van on the roads of many countries. All rather more than the cinq plombiers Richard once had in mind!

Chapter 9

People who are busiest get the most done

'I say to my children that it's not the taking part that counts – it's the winning. I do believe you should try your hardest in whatever you do. I know it sounds a bit scary, but my mentality in business extends to everything.'

Contrary to the first eight chapters of this book, Richard Harpin actually has a life outside work. He works hard, but is just as dedicated to establishing the same stable kind of family life he himself enjoyed.

When Richard and wife Kate got married in July 1997, they spent their first three years of marriage in Nottingham, just over an hour from HomeServe's Walsall HQ. Then, as their first child arrived, thoughts turned to a more rural environment – and there was only one county in the frame.

'Yorkshire, because that's where Kate's parents lived, and still do. We recognised that I'd be travelling more and more, and it was important to have a base. I was keen to go back to Yorkshire because that was where I was born and where I'd spent the first four or five years of my life. I still see myself as a northerner and wanted my children to have roots.'

High up on the wish-list was 'a nice village, with a school and a church and a pub' – and they found their ideal house on the front page of the Yorkshire Post in the first week of looking. It had been owned by the village doctor and had been a vicarage at some point, 'obviously when the clergy were paid a bit more than they are now! It's our ideal house, with just less than an acre of land, a nice family home.'

Interestingly, the purchase went through in the space of just one week – and with sealed bids the chosen system, and five other people interested in buying it, Harpin concedes his negotiating skills failed to secure a bargain. 'We overpaid to get the house, but when you see the ideal house you've got to go for it. We managed to negotiate a price to make sure it was accepted before the sealed bids – we didn't want to lose it, we wanted to make sure they'd accept our offer rather than taking pot luck.

'Once we'd bought it, we put our house in Nottingham on the market. We decided not to rent it out and, as I'd promised my chairman, Brian Whitty, and his wife they could come to dinner in Nottingham, I thought we'd better invite them quickly. I had to take down the "For Sale" sign before he arrived because I wanted to explain why I was moving even further away from the office in Walsall when he thought that Nottingham had been far too far away in the first place!'

Richard had hoped to be able to commute by train, but in 2000 found himself stuck in-between stations during floods. 'I thought I'd have to find some other way. So I used firemen, on their off shift, to drive me. I bought an old long-wheelbase Mercedes that had been in Dubai and based it in Walsall. The firemen would drive up and pick me up at 5.30am in the morning, I'd stop off at the gym en route, and then in the evening I'd leave the office at 5.00 or 5.30pm and have a two-and-a-half hour journey back home. I didn't spend a lot of time with my two older children because they'd be in bed by the time I got home.

'I was also spending quite a lot of time in Walsall in those days because the international businesses hadn't been established. It was pretty grim spending five hours a day in a car. Eight or more hours a day in the office and then another five hours working in the back of the car was too much… I always used to be car-sick as a child, but I had to train myself to be able to read and work properly in the back of the car.

'So it was great when I could afford a helicopter, did my training and got my licence – I only had the car in the morning, but I used the helicopter in the evening and it made a big difference to my life. It meant that our third child has seen a lot more of me particularly since I swapped my fair-weather helicopter, a Robinson 44, for a Twin Squirrel. I have a fully instrument-rated pilot alongside me to make sure I never get into difficulties and can use it every day.'

His rotary-wing acquisition fulfilled that childhood ambition stirred when he used to watch Lord Hanson arrive by helicopter to have Sunday lunch with his parents. When the Squirrel is out of action for servicing, Richard borrows another from ex-England striker Michael Owen, and vice versa.

'Helicopters are good for getting to race meetings and Michael's a keen racehorse owner. He's nearly as sold on them as I am!'

Harpin learned to fly ten years ago. 'I had a particular fascination for helicopters but it was logical to do fixed-wing first as it's a bit cheaper. I went on to helicopters two years later.' His new acquisition can fly in bad weather and poor visibility 'and that makes all the difference. I had to poach Steve Beaumont, the captain of the Yorkshire Air Ambulance, who had done four thousand military hours and was used to flying at night and in bad weather.

The helicopter means I can attend two meetings in different parts of the country and still usually make it home to spend time with my children – although, given the nature of my job, it is not always possible.'

He only uses it the one way 'because I haven't found a way that I can get through my working day and deal with my in-tray without getting up at 5.00 in the morning, and I feel that if I didn't get into my car at 5.30 and do my in-tray and stop at the gym, my exercise levels would suffer, I'd get out of bed later and I wouldn't be as productive.

'But I am an early starter, and I want to make sure that I'm putting in as many hours as I can to keep this business growing as fast and as successfully as it can, alongside the team that are actually running the business now, the three chief executives…'

By the time Richard Harpin arrives at his Walsall head office, he will have worked on his in-tray for two and a half hours. 'I always say "The day when I get through my in-tray is the day I give up business".' The first half-hour in Walsall is spent with his two secretaries Jayne Neal and Diane Saunders and is as invaluable as they themselves have proved.

'They've both worked for me for a long time – Di for over ten years – and to work for me and put up with talking to me and seeing me most working days for that long must be a remarkable achievement. They split the roles well between them, so Jayne does the diary, the planning for meetings and the preparation for meetings, all the complicated travel arrangements and so on, while Di does the follow-ups from those meetings, all emails and researches new ideas.'

Harpin is keen to give the people who facilitate his working life the credit they deserve – especially after a negative comment once made in a 360 degree review claimed that 'Richard Harpin is too busy to be nice'. 'I think what that meant,' he grimaces good-naturedly, 'was that I was always on to my next meeting or my next project, and it is important always to try and have a bit of spare time to say "Here's what's happening in the business, thanks for all your hard work and support… what are your feelings and what are you up to?" I hope I took that negative comment on board, and said to myself that I did need to make a bit more time so people didn't always feel I was rushing from one thing to the next.'

That may apply to his private office. But does Richard Harpin think the rank and file in the HomeServe call centre perceive him as someone who's reasonably approachable, or just see him for a couple of seconds passing through as 'that bloke who hops in the helicopter at the end of the day'?

> 'Hopefully, people will think that I am very hands-on... While I've adopted a means of transport that looks very high-flying, I'm down-to-earth, prepared to roll up my sleeves and I'll walk round the call centre and get a dozen or so people in for a sandwich lunch to get their point of view on things and listen to their comments. Pressures on your time mean that you can never be as approachable as you want to be, but I'm always out to encourage people to make contact if they've got an idea, or they think there's an area of the business where we're going wrong that I'm not aware of.'

In the very early days, Richard physically sat in one of their seats and sampled their daily regime himself. But he had to be restrained. 'Given that most people would describe me as a very good salesman, and given that I think that when somebody says "No" that means "Yes"' eventually, there was always a worry that when I was actually taking live calls myself and selling a policy, I'd be over-selling the benefits...there was a certain nervousness. I don't do it now because I think it's actually better to listen to others doing it, to get a feel for the best way to sell – and there's a lot of people in the business who are much better salesmen for our products than I am!'

One thing he still makes a point of doing is sitting and listening to actual calls in the HomeServe call centres. And he has even been known to call up customers personally to deal with any grievance and assure them that the man at the top is not only approachable but also listening. 'We had a board meeting in Preston recently where we spent an hour-and-a-half on the phones listening in to how we're performing. In my briefcase there's a CD of some of the calls from the Walsall operation which is concerned with the One Contact initiative – converting emergency calls from non-members into getting them to buy a policy as part of the resolution. Those are calls that I will listen to on my way into the office tomorrow morning.'

Maximising the use of his time is crucial to Richard Harpin's working life. He even believes that, 'if you really work at it, you can cram two-and-a-half lives into one. The people who are busiest always seem to be the people who get the most done…it's constant thinking and working, the same as if I'm on a train, it's solid work.

'The only time I ever fell asleep in the back of a car was when I was in a pre-booked taxi in London, and I woke up about an hour later with the driver asking which terminal I wanted. "That's odd," I thought. "I'm sure there's only one terminal at (private airstrip) Biggin Hill…"

'We'd arrived at Heathrow – there had been two taxi bookings, one for me and one for an American guy, and we'd each got in the wrong car. I'd been taken to Heathrow, and he'd ended up at Biggin Hill. Fortunately, with a private plane, it meant I was an hour-and-a-quarter late but didn't miss my flight, which the American unfortunately did… So that taught me never to go to sleep in the back of a car, but to work like mad!'

Head of Home Service US Jonathan King had heard Richard explain his time-management theories at HomeServe meetings and has taken many to heart. 'He's talked about things like always trying to use the five or ten minutes between the end of one meeting and the beginning of the next – it's very easy to wander around, make a cup of coffee or have a pee, but actually there's a lot you can get done in five minutes. And if you make sure you use every single bit of the day, and don't stop, you can be so much more productive.

'Another thing is to draw yourself a four-box grid. The horizontal axis represents the importance of the task, and the vertical axis represents the urgency of the task. The urgency goes from high to low and the importance from low to high, so the top left box is high urgency/low importance. Richard says too many people spend too much time in that box, and that what you should always be striving to do is the jobs in the bottom right box, the high-importance/low-urgency jobs, as these are the ones that often get left behind. The constant stream of things you work through during the day tends to stop you doing these, stops you from thinking about the future, thinking about where you're going next and what are the big issues you've got to deal with… I think that's a very useful thing to remind yourself of from time to time.'

Richard doesn't have a computer on his desk, and that's another habit King has adopted for himself 'because it's very distracting. One of the things that can happen is that e-mail and its content ends up driving your personal agenda – it drives how you use your day in responding to it. I'm really shocked that so many people, even quite senior people, see their job as sitting in front of a PC sending and responding to e-mail.

'I had one guy I employed over here, and the moment I knew he wasn't right for the business was the day he walked into my office at 11 o'clock in the morning and said that the e-mail system hadn't been working for the last two hours so he hadn't been able to do any work.'

Richard Harpin's weeks are nothing if not busy. Monday is always spent in head office in Walsall. Here he meets Jon Florsheim, the UK CEO, for a one to one, and the same with Martin Bennett his CFO. Then there is a weekly one-hour conference call at 4pm for all three CEOs plus him and his Chief Financial Officer to review the issues and opportunities from last week's performance. They review the take-up from sales calls, examining the number made, response rates, the number of complaints and the quantity of no-quibble payouts made to unsatisfied customers. They also run through progress on the 'big ideas' to grow the business.

Typically he will spend at least a day a week in London attending back-to-back meetings in the city and meeting his shareholders. 'Then I will try and spend my time around the businesses. I spend quite a lot of time on European business development helping to make acquisitions happen when we've found the right companies in existing or new countries, persuading their owners that joining HomeServe is a good idea.

'The US is a big opportunity as well as continental Europe, so now I aim to be there every four to six weeks. Typically I would go on a Tuesday morning and fly back overnight on a Thursday evening so I get, even in that week, a Monday and a Friday in the UK. Straight off the plane and into the office on a Friday morning.

'I'm someone who can sleep anywhere so I get a good night's sleep overnight and I've worked out if I do three days in the US and two days in the UK I actually get a sixth day free! Six for the price of five – if Concorde existed today I wouldn't use it because it wouldn't be as efficient!

'I work solidly on the flight out on Tuesday. People always say they've never seen anybody working solidly on their in-tray for eight and a half hours on the flight. I've never ever watched an in-flight film. I work constantly and have a 24-28-hour day on the day I fly to the US because I then do a full day's work when I get there. So that's how you get six days for the price of five...'

Brother Stephen confirms Richard has 'always been absolutely driven in everything he's done, and he puts everything into it – whatever he does, he's driven to do it, and I think that the combination of always looking for an edge, seeing how you can beat the competition and employing people who can make it happen has stood him in very good stead.' As for family life, 'I read once in the newspaper that he gets home twice a week to put the children to bed. But I'm not sure that's true...'

Richard does his best to achieve the right work/life balance, both for himself and the people working for the company. 'For me, the thing that does most to maintain the balance is the helicopter, which is my way of relaxing. Flying, and especially flying home, is a great passion of mine – but it means I can work hard and still get home one or two days a week for tea-time and bath-time with my young children.

'Family, home and children are really important to me. And though I don't always get the balance right, I know I have a very supportive wife who tries to help me do so...' Once he's home in the evening and the children are in bed he has supper with Kate before he allows himself to relax and read the newspapers. Then, and only then, does he check the company's share price, on his BlackBerry. It is a mistake to worry about the share price rather than the customers, he says. 'That's when things go wrong.' Bedtime is 11pm.

Does he dream about work? Probably, but there are limits to even a workaholic's obsession. 'I never stop thinking about work, but I do stop myself from working at weekends. So although the next idea is always running around in my head, weekends are for family and for doing the normal sort of stuff that fathers working 9-5 can perhaps take for granted. For me, I can never take for granted I'll be home at 6 o'clock, or with my children at weekends, so having that time with them is a treat…

'I'd also like to think that I'm true to my roots. Living in North Yorkshire, having been born in West Yorkshire, I hope that one day I'll be seen as one of the few Yorkshiremen that have made it big internationally in the way that Lord Hanson did. It's a source of a great deal of pride that I can live in a beautiful house, in a lovely village with a vibrant village life, and combine that with an international business career with a great set of people at HomeServe.

'I think you've got to get a good balance in life between work and play. I work hard and play hard. I don't work at weekends as a general rule and I try not to do too much corporate hospitality – being away at a football or a rugby game at the weekend – because I think that's family time. That's about home, friends, village life and supporting the children, ferrying them around to their various activities and spending time with Kate.

'I don't play golf now because that's too much time away, and I try to keep my weekend activities to the things the children want to do.'

When it comes to his own children, he is happy for them to follow their own muse. ‘I’d like to think my entrepreneurial skills will rub off on one of my three children, the one that really wants to follow that career path in whatever line of business they choose to set up or run. I’m sure the other two will probably go off and do something that’s not entrepreneurial, but suits them.’

The most important thing, he says, is that they’ll have ‘even more choices than I had. I was very grateful to my parents that they put the small amount of spare money that they had into private education for my brother and me rather than holidays abroad, which stopped at the age of seven or eight until university. They couldn’t afford to do both… My children are very fortunate in that they have all of that, and really the only worry is that they may take it for granted. It’s hard to keep the balance and explain that not every dad has a helicopter that they fly back from work in every night, or a private aeroplane, and getting that sense of balance between that and the day-to-day stuff like fixing their bikes, washing cars and all that sort of stuff.

Asked whether Kate understands the pressures of business life or has learned to live with it, he laughs: ‘She’s learned to live with me! I think I’m probably a particularly difficult individual to live with because of my extreme A-type risk personality, because of the level of determination I put into my business. Hopefully, I put the same level of effort into the things I do at home with my family.

When it comes to his own recreation, Richard Harpin is fanatical. His annual ‘boys’ ski week’ includes friends from all walks of life. ‘He’s never changed,’ long-time friend Simon Blunt confirms, ‘though obviously he flies there in a different kind of aircraft now… Everything Richard does in life is a competition, but in a nice way. We used to play tennis and squash and things, and whatever it was,

he'd eventually beat me – he beat me at tennis, he beat me at squash and he beat me in business! The only thing he hasn't overtaken me in so far is the skiing…

'The boys' ski week every year is made up of a dozen 'lads' from all walks of life and all sorts of backgrounds. The group has split into two or three – you've got the "café latte" group, who like to sit around and drink coffee everywhere, and then you've got the A-Team, which is myself, Harpin and Middleton, and Richard's still number two! I've got to start doing some training this year, because he's getting very close!

'The A-team go off-piste,' Simon continues. 'We have an off-piste guide, and we do some pretty tough stuff – he'll overtake me not necessarily because of his technique or his ability, but because of his lack of fear. He'll go off and do things I hesitate over, simply because "Blunty won't do it"… He's got the bottle to do it, and it's all down to having no fear.

'The only time I've seen "total no fear" is when we went fox-hunting once, charging across this moor that had logs everywhere – if you'd fallen off, if you didn't kill yourself you'd have seriously hurt yourself. He was out of control, well we both were, but he'd told the guy we'd hired the horses from that we were both experienced riders. We weren't, and they'd given us these two huge beasts… We weren't good enough to ride these horses, they were charging along and Richard was laughing. He slipped round the neck of the horse and was holding on – if he'd dropped on the ground he'd have been trampled. That's when I realised that the guy has no fear…'

Richard started skiing relatively late in life, 'in my early twenties because the choice for my parents was either holidays aboard or private education. My parents chose the latter, which was the right decision. I couldn't do both, which is why I started to ride horses, starting to go skiing when I left home. And there was a bit more money around to do it – I could finance it myself. I loved skiing and got to the stage where I was skiing off-piste where there are no lifts, no people. It's like being on the moon, or what I would imagine being on the moon is! It's very quiet, all you can see is beautiful snow and mountains and rocks. So the best way to go where there are no lifts and is more than an hour's walk – I'm only prepared to walk an hour for a decent off-piste run – is heli-skiing.

'One time I was heli-skiing with some good friends. One, Steve Gray, who was doing it for the first time got out of the helicopter. It was very icy and he put his skis on. The other two of us and the guide saw him slipping very quickly towards a sheer drop – we thought he was a goner. The guide just managed to grab his jacket and hold him before he went over. The whole thing took about 15 seconds. When we got back to our girlfriends and wives at lunchtime Steve said "Darling, all I could think about in those last 15 seconds when I knew I was going to die was you." He told us earlier on the way down it was the regrets on his share portfolio! My last thoughts would have been "What a pity…I've got so much left to achieve."'

Newcastle pal Geoff Gillie has been on more than 30 holidays with Richard since chasing those light-fingered Spaniards of Chapter 1. 'We've done around 15 summer holidays, and we've been skiing about 20 times – I've roomed with him on a lot of those occasions, but I've never seen him sleep! He's always the last one out of the club, though he's not a big drinker, and always the last one to bed. When you wake up in the morning he's already up, and he's on his computer or his phone doing his next deal. And the likelihood is that he's checking out some potential business opportunity, because someone has tipped him off about something the night before.

'He takes his business brain on holiday,' Geoff continues, 'he's always got something on the go. On every chair-lift, he's on the phone, but he enjoys that, that's what he is. When we go skiing, he'll be talking to Jeremy (Middleton) about how they're going to do this, or how they're going to do that, and over what timescale…

'The conversation normally runs along these lines: Richard will say "I'm going to do this, or I'm going to do that", and Jeremy will say "But Richard, can you really do that, and how long will it take?" to which Richard answers "Oh, yeah, I can do that in six months'. Jeremy will say "Can you really do that in six months? I think it'll take you a year", but Richard's always adamant he can turn these things around, he's like that all the time...'

So, Richard Harpin, the question remains – why must your pastimes be challenging? Why not take up bowls, chess, cricket or billiards as most forty-somethings would?

'I say to my children that it's not the taking part that counts – it's the winning. I do believe you should try your hardest in whatever you do. I know it sounds a bit scary, but my mentality in business extends to everything.'

Chapter 10

If it isn't making money, don't persevere

'It's better to stand up and admit your mistakes, do it earlier rather than later, be bold about taking a write-off, and get on and focus attention back on the core business.'

Even now, three decades into his entrepreneurial career, Richard Harpin sees his early stint at Procter and Gamble as 'a great learning experience. It taught me marketing and to see things from a consumer point of view, as well as introducing me to a big network of people.'

He was therefore pleased to be invited in 2004 to present the HomeServe Story to the association of former employees that meets every Christmas in London to hear an invited speaker's business story. 'It was a hard audience to speak to,' he confessed. 'I never thought I would be back giving it. I remember the early days of going to those dos. They're full of management consultants, people trying to flog their own services, looking for big PLC clients –

which I wasn't. As soon as I told people I ran a plumbing business they ran a mile! They sat on a different table and said they were never going to sell management consultancy to me…

'It was nice to come back knowing that HomeServe had become successful and I had been invited to give the HomeServe story to that audience. It's a good network. People who know me would say one of my big strengths is networking and one of my philosophies is always look after everybody the same way. Always remember the people you've worked with on the way up. Hopefully I'm only a couple of rungs up the ladder on the way up.'

The latest threat to HomeServe's business was the proposal that water companies take over responsibility, in 2011, for the section of shared sewer pipe between a customer's property boundary up to where it connects to the main water company's sewer in the middle of the main road. As ever, this threat was being treated as an opportunity.

Analysts in the City thought this could be a problem that threatened the HomeServe business model and that HomeServe would no longer be required… In fact HomeServe covers all the pipe from the house up to the customer's boundary.

Harpin soon realised that this was another opportunity for HomeServe because it highlighted the fact that people don't know what they are, and are not, responsible for. 'Our marketing is not glossy, hard-sell marketing, it points out customer responsibilities with diagrams and pictures. What we want to do is to tell customers that there's a threat, because they could have a big repair bill. So why don't we cover that free for the next 12 months, write to customers under our water-company partner names, and tell them to call HomeServe if they'd like this free cover and then aim to upsell them to a higher level of cover thus turning a threat into an opportunity.

The future for HomeServe involves embracing technology, and mobile phones and e-mail will be increasingly integrated into their marketing plan. Tests on e-mail marketing in 2009 achieved about 0.6 per cent take-up in France – a good response rate given the minimal cost of sending an e-mail, so e-mail marketing will play a large part in HomeServe's future plans. And that's not all, as Richard reveals.

'We're also quite a way down the road to developing an all-singing, all-dancing website which will offer customers a complete service when getting a repair done, and will get their job request, at a fixed price, to the engineer who will call the customer back within 15 minutes and confirm their arrival time to deal with the emergency. There's a version of that being tested in the midlands as part of the One Contact pay-on-use service, and we see a huge opportunity to roll that out not just in the UK but across all of our international markets once fully proven out in the UK.'

HomeServe has now been going for 15 years, and Richard Harpin feels more excited now than at any stage in its history. 'There are more opportunities, in more countries - we're developing our appliance warranty business internationally and the key thing is, we've got 'first mover' – advantage. We've got critical mass, we need to make it happen quickly. It's not about looking back and saying 'We've been quite successful so far', it's about keeping that momentum going, and if we start to slow down or congratulate ourselves on how well we've done so far, then we'll lose it.

'It's also about maintaining that sense of entrepreneurial spirit and the culture of discipline, which is about the testing, and making sure that however big we eventually become, we still think small. I talked about thinking big earlier, but this is about the company thinking as a small company would – being fleet of foot, fast moving, and getting things done quickly. The pace of the business hasn't changed, it's still very ambitious with lots of things going on.'

Acquisitions made on the home emergency side of the business – including Highway, Sergon, Improveline and Chemdry – failed to deliver the hoped-for profits, and in 2009 it was announced that these would be sold off at a loss of £97 million. Harpin holds his hands up to the fact that this has been his biggest mistake.

'We spent £130 million of borrowed money and Homeserve profit to go and buy a number of businesses. It didn't work out, and we had to write off the best part of £100 million…not only that, but there was the opportunity cost of diverting management time and energy into developing that operation at the expense of growing our core membership business even faster. Having gone down that cul-de-sac, the important thing is to recognise that, put your hands up, apologise to shareholders that the money has been wasted. It's better to stand up and admit your mistakes, do it earlier rather than later,

'Every so often you need to question things and say "What should be on the Not To Do list?", and actually, when we stood up and said we were sorry and took the £100 million write-off, the share price went up, not down, which rewarded us for being honest and getting our focus back on the core business where we can add significantly more shareholder value.'

Chairman Brian Whitty concurs. 'With HomeServe emergency services, the issue was that we were not in control of our own customer base and were reliant on a number of large insurers. A couple of years ago, because of the floods, they've had to look seriously at their cost base and it has come back on us. What we've learned is that we have to be in control of the end customer relationship. The relationship with the householder is the critical part of our model.'

In Richard Harpin's view, 'Nobody should be criticised or penalised for making mistakes – it's a shame it was such a big mistake, but the important thing is not to make the same mistakes again. We have to make sure that in future we only do the things that really enhance the model, we focus on our competencies and where we add value in the business, and we look at the things that allow us to grow the business faster by concentrating on the core activities that really add shareholder value.'

Long-time friend Geoff Gillie sees this as a key trait. 'He's wrong plenty of times, but he knows when to stop when he is. He'll look to see if he can fix something, but if his investigations tell him he can't, he'll pull the plug and close the file. If something isn't making enough money, he won't persevere with it. He has now learnt that…'

The man brought in to turn things around at HomeServe Emergency Services was Ian Carlisle. 'It was typical Richard… He rang me on my mobile - I still can't work out how he got the number - and said "I hear you've done great things at Autoglass and I need someone like you in my business." I found out afterwards he'd done the research and identified the kind of person he wanted, then made the approach himself.'

We met the following week. He said to me 'I know where I want to take the business, and I know what I'm thinking of doing is right, but I've basically gone off and bought an operational company, paid a lot of money for it, and in the six months that I've had it it's gone backwards at a rate of knots…

'It was the right business to buy, but he hadn't really thought through what you do with it once you've bought it, and it became a scramble after the event to catch up. There was all this visionary stuff - "We're going to be the name in everyone's home, the AA for the home" - but the first thing they had to do was overcome this big issue… I suppose that situation showed the best and the worst of him… He very much gets the idea in his head and he's off and running before it's fully developed.

'You've got to earn Richard's trust, and I think you either get that very early on, or you never get it. Certainly his top team is there because he trusts them. Once he trusts you, the accountabilities for the businesses that you run are with you. I think that's a key ingredient of why entrepreneurs run great businesses - they make sure they get strong people in to do the things in the business they're not good at.'

Ian Carlisle was at HomeServe for five-and-a-half years, and enjoyed the experience despite the outcome. A number of things rubbed off. 'Richard taught me that you can go faster than you thought you could go, and you can achieve more than you thought you could achieve… Also that you should never let your ambition be curtailed by risk. And the whole thing about the empowering of people you trust…all those things came out of working with Richard.'

The decision to dispose of HomeServe Emergency Services was, Carlisle says, 'absolutely right. The market went from looking for partners that can add value to the insurance market to a looser, more transactional relationship, even less caring about its supply chain. I think there was a conflict with what HomeServe was and where it could potentially go. I think for Richard it's about sticking to the basics. Don't try to do too much…the membership model is the core model for the group, and making that international is, I think, where he should keep it focused.'

Former headhunter Joel Barnett shares his view as to where HomeServe should be heading, but with a twist.

'I've got a very controversial view of what they should be doing, but then who am I to have such a view? So you have to take this in context, and not regard this as what I think they have to do… If I were in charge, I'd probably be more inclined to flatline the profits and re-invest in growth. 'Rather than focus on growing profit every year and delivering that commitment to the City, I would take a slightly longer-term view.'

Brother Stephen sees no change in his brother's future course. 'If I asked Richard where he's going to go in the future, he'd say "FTSE 100, and in order to do that I need to spend the following amount in the following markets over the following time period, and that will produce earnings of x at the cost of y, and that will get me into the FTSE 100…", and he'd be relatively black and white about that, totally unfazed, and that's what's going to happen... and I suspect that's exactly what's going to happen. I can't imagine him ever packing it in, actually.

'That's partly because he knows the business inside out, partly because he's absolutely driven to make a success of it, and the definition of success is "bigger than it is now", and then "bigger than it was". I can't see him starting another business, because to do that he'd have to retire from the business he's looking to make bigger, and I can't see him slowing down - I think he'll keel over before he slows down, the business is his life...

'I think he will still be moving as fast in ten years' time as he is now - just can't see him slowing down... in fact, if I go down to his house, we'll be sitting there chatting away in the evening, he'll be manic, and then eventually, he'll be sitting there asleep - it's all or nothing. He'll be frantically doing something, he'll be off to play tennis, or organising squash for the village, refurbishing the squash courts or something, and he'll do all that and then you'll see him after dinner and he'll be up surfing... it's quite extraordinary, really. I don't think I've ever seen him sit back in a chair, unless he's reading a business book or something...

'It's all or nothing, there's never a moment's relaxation, and he'll just be out for the count, fallen asleep. But if you wake him up, he'll stand up immediately and go off and do something...'

Meanwhile the UK membership business that provides the vast majority of the group's profits, is under the guidance of ex-Sky man Jon Florsheim. The warranty business has been amalgamated into membership, and Richard sees this as the way forward.

'I think it's about working with the team on developing the next part of the model. Although HomeServe is now, and will remain, focused on membership, we need to look at how we get it from five countries to, say, 28 countries. We've gone from organic set-up to buy-and-build, and there will be work on developing that model – there's a very exciting new element to the business model, which is not just about utility home assistance but about a membership scheme for electrical and gas appliances. That's a key part of the model that we now want to develop internationally.

'Our aim is to start working with major appliance manufacturers, particularly the boiler and washing machine manufacturers outside the UK. All we need to do is prove to them that we can do a fantastic job in a couple of countries in continental Europe, and there'll be no reason why they won't say "Well, actually, we'd like you to do this in every country in which we operate." The scale of that opportunity and thinking through how we would make that happen is really exciting.

For pal Geoff Gillie, there's no end in sight. 'I was talking to Richard a couple of years ago, when he started to get into the tens of millions, and I said "Where does all this end - you've now got more money than you could ever need, so where does it all end?" He said, "It doesn't end - it hasn't even started yet!"

'He motivates people by leading by example. I've never worked with him financially, but I can imagine his approach would be to say "Look, I think this is how we should do this" rather than "I want you to do that", and I think that comes naturally to him. If there's anything going on, he's always sticking his nose in at the beginning, and if there's something to do, he's the one who's doing it.

'He's happy to have everyone else doing it as well, but he leads by example, and he's the first one into everything. It doesn't matter whether there's a business to set up, or an investigation into whether the business works - even when we were younger and single, things like "There's a group of girls there, how are we going to get in to chat them up?" - it's all the same to him, whatever it might be. He's tireless, really. I don't know where he gets his energy… I've never really come across anybody else that has the energy he has, but he seems always to have had it.

'If he jumps in a swimming pool, he'll have to swim a mile. He'll do 25 lengths, while most of us would jump in the swimming pool and do a couple of lengths before taking it easy and lying on our backs. Richard has to prove himself.'

Richard Harpin returned to his alma mater, York University, in 2007 to open their enterprise centre. 'If we'd had the centre in my day back in '83-'84, it would have helped a lot. It does show the tremendous way enterprise has developed and I remember some people at school despising me because I was making money and you shouldn't be making money at school out of other pupils in those days. I think today that would be turned on its head and people admire enterprise.'

It was the meeting with Joanna Lumley at the Entrepreneur Of The Year 2008 award ceremony that led to Richard taking an interest in the Prince's Trust in backing young entrepreneurs. 'She wrote to me and said you must become involved in the Prince's Trust, she's one of their ambassadors. I recently got an invitation from Prince Charles to have lunch with him. Unfortunately it was on a Monday and that's my day in Walsall looking at the business results for the previous week. Not for anybody would I not want to do my Monday in the business so I turned him down – then read in the newspaper the following Sunday that seven selected people had been invited, and of course my name wasn't there!

'I thought maybe I should have gone, so I did go and find out about the Prince's Trust as I thought it might link in with my encouraging more young entrepreneurs. I will get involved in doing something there.'

Richard typically sees the recession of 2008-09 as an opportunity for those who wish to become their own bosses. 'I think there will, out of necessity, be many of those people who find themselves in the unfortunate position of being unemployed. Instead of saying I'm on the scrapheap, maybe they can turn that bad news into doing something they'd always wanted to do – setting up their own business.'

If risk-taking is what separates entrepreneurs from the rest of the world, then anyone who's unemployed arguably has less of a risk to take than if they were in employment. When Richard set up his first full-time business it was with the backing of a business partner, Jeremy Middleton, who stayed in his existing job as he was the higher earner.

'We said we've got enough money put aside to fund the business and pay my salary for two years so there wasn't extreme hardship there. But the money would have run out after two years – in fact, it ran out quicker. You've got to take that leap of faith, the equivalent of jumping out of the helicopter, and if you don't there's no rewards. If you're already standing on the skid of the helicopter cos you're unemployed you may as well jump.'

Alan Middleton, CEO of PA Consulting, is one of Britain's top business analysts. He met Richard Harpin at the Stanford University course mentioned in Chapter 1 and came away with some interesting perspectives on the man and his business.

'The Stanford executive programme was a taster of all aspects of running a business, if that makes sense, marketing, finance and so on, and Richard spent time applying the thinking from the course, but also taking time out to think about where his business should go next. He and I spent a lot of time kicking general ideas around.'

Middleton feels it's a credit to Harpin that he admits his weaknesses. 'He's a very confident man, and he knows he's strong in certain areas…but there were certain areas he'd never bothered with in which he wanted to gain a greater understanding. He was particularly keen to do one of the modules on the course covering strategy and positioning, setting out strategy for business, and I believe he took a great deal from that. The guy who ran that course was called Robert Burgelman, a very good professor who has some alternative views on how you go about doing this, and I think Richard found that very interesting.

'I find Richard to be one of the more interesting entrepreneurs that you'll meet. He understands his strengths and he understands his weaknesses, and he exercises that understanding to the full. It's quite rare to meet someone with his energy, his enthusiasm and his success – he just continues to burn bright and incredibly energetically, always thinking about the customer, always thinking about the marketing. And I love the fact that he doesn't spend a great deal of time worrying about all the internal workings of his business – he simply finds the very best people that he can and gets them to run those for him.

'For me, Richard is the perfect example of a man who knows what he's good at, does that well, then hires brilliant people and doesn't feel threatened by them. There are many people like him – the Richard Bransons of this world – and I think he's got that same kind of style, that same kind of drive and unrelenting ambition, but at the same time, he doesn't feel the need to over-manage or overpower the people he's brought in.'

Middleton believes Richard was born with his dogged, energetic qualities and developed them further. 'It's hard to learn to be as charismatic as he is… He's learned not to fear failure, which I think is a great asset. He decides what he's going to do, and once he's decided, he goes off and does it. Many of us would worry about whether it's the right decision, whether it'll be a success or a failure, but Richard pursues the things he thinks are right with unrelenting optimism – and, more often than not I understand, he and his team are successful.'

While Richard himself cannot see further than a future at HomeServe, Alan Middleton would like to see him spreading himself around. 'I think it would be easy for Richard to spend the next ten years building more success around the HomeServe model, but I think that entrepreneurial, market-facing, client-facing characters like him are few and far between. Before he hangs up his spurs it would be great to see him applying his strengths to other British organisations and helping to make them successful.

'Richard's in what you might call the mass customer service/retail sector, and that's an area in the UK at the moment that certainly needs good, visionary leadership and a really good understanding of how to serve customers well. I'm not going to name names…but I can see Richard doing that, whether as CEO or in a non-executive role, and I think he's got a lot to add to British GDP.'

With a story as fast-moving as this, things have been happening even as the book was being prepared for print. HomeServe have a new CFO (Chief Financial Officer), Martin Bennett. He had been with the company for six years and was previously Finance Director of the UK membership division. 'Martin has already had a positive impact, making stuff happen,' said Richard Harpin who anticipates further internal promotions in the future.

The emergency services division was finally disposed of, allowing the group to concentrate on its higher-margin, higher-growth membership business and this was well received by the City and shareholders. Having doubled since Christmas 2008, the share price continues its upward movement. The regular 18-monthly meeting of analysts and shareholders to review the business was held at the end of September and the feedback was that HomeServe was looking good to deliver continued growth.

Finally, Richard handed over his Entrepreneur Of The Year crown in early October to Michael Spencer of Icap. As at Monte Carlo, he took the stage in HomeServe cap and boot covers, with monkey wrench in hand, to laughter and applause. Now on the judging panel, he has the chance to feed his knowledge and experience back into the competition in forthcoming years.

The unsung hero of the HomeServe part of the story, whom Richard has worked with for twelve years, is Brian Whitty. "He was my Chief Executive at South Staffordshire Group in the earlier days of HomeServe and became Chairman of HomeServe when we demerged in 2004. Brian has really helped me by acting as a challenger of my less good ideas, a sounding board and mentor". Many successful entrepreneurs will have had a "Brian" providing invaluable support.

Let's leave the last word, as ever, to the man himself. 'I still feel, even today, 16 years into the biggest business I've ever run, that we've still only just started…we're still only in five countries, and we can be a truly worldwide business, so there's still a lot to come. It should get easier and easier as time goes by, because we have better people and more resources at our disposal, so getting from £100 million profit to £200 million should be far easier than it was to get to £100 million in the first place.

> 'I've got no intention of moving on and doing something else, because I love what I'm doing and I still feel that I'm adding some value to the business. I've got plenty of other things that I'll do one day, and I want to make sure that I put some time into helping the next generation of entrepreneurs – and more apprentices to become the skilled workforce of the future.

'– plus I've got some other business ideas that I'll work on one day.'

Appendix 1

Recommended Reading

Top Man: How Philip Green Built His High Street Empire
Stewart Lansley & Andy Forrester
Aurum Press Ltd (2006) ISBN: 978-1845131685

Business Stripped Bare: Adventures of a Global Entrepreneur
by Sir Richard Branson
Virgin Books (2009) ISBN: 978-0753515037

Jeff Bezos: Business Executive and Founder of Amazon.Com (Ferguson Career Biographies)
by Bernard Ryan
Facts on File Inc (2005) ISBN: 978-0816058907

Formula One: the Business of Winning
by Russell Hotten
Orion (1998) ISBN: 978-0752812076

The Chocolate Wars:
Inside the Secret Worlds of Mars and Hershey
by Joel G. Brenner
HarperCollins Business (2000) ISBN: 978-0006532392

Work in Progress
by Michael D. Eisner , Tony Schwartz
Hyperion Books (1999) ISBN: 978-0786885077

Sky High, The Inside Story of BSkyB:
by Mathew Horsman
ISBN: 0752811967

Inside Intel: Andy Grove and the Rise of the World's Most Powerful Chip Company
by Tim Jackson
Plume Books (1998) ISBN: 978-0452276437

Bloomberg by Bloomberg
by Michael Bloomberg
John Wiley & Sons (2001) ISBN: 978-0471208884

Freak or Unique?: Chris Evans Story
by David Jones
HarperCollins Publishers Ltd (1997) ISBN: 978-0006530176

Call Me Ted: The Autobiography of the Extraordinary Business Leader and Founder of CNN
by Ted Turner
Sphere (2008) ISBN: 978-1847442796

Buffett: The Making of an American Capitalist
by Roger Lowenstein
Weidenfeld & Nicolson (1996) SBN-13: 978-0297817055

Direct From Dell: Strategies that Revolutionized an Industry
by Michael Dell
Profile Business (2000) ISBN: 978-1861975577

Business at the Speed of Thought: Succeeding in the Digital Economy (Penguin Business Library)
by Bill Gates
Penguin; (2000) ISBN: 978-0140283129

Jack Welch and the GE Way: Management Insights and Leadership Secrets of the Legendary CEO
by Robert Slater
McGraw-Hill Education (2002) ISBN: 978-0071380485

Obsession: The Lives and Times of Calvin Klein
by Gaines
Birch Lane Press (1994) ISBN: 978-1559722353

Who Says Elephants Can't Dance?: How I Turned Around IBM
by Louis Gerstner
HarperCollins Publishers Ltd (2003) ISBN: 978-0007170876

Design for Six Sigma: The Revolutionary Process for Achieving Extraordinary Profits
by Subir Chowdhury
Kaplan Business (2005) ISBN: 978-1419526817

The Spirit to Serve: Marriot's Way
by J W Marriott Jr , Kathi Ann Brown
HarperCollins (1997) ISBN: 978-0887309915

The Prince
by Niccolo Machiavelli , Tim Parks
Penguin Classics (2009) ISBN: 978-1846140440

Cold Steel: Lakshmi Mittal and the Multi-billion-dollar Battle for a Global Empire
by Tim Bouquet, Byron Ousey
Abacus (2009) ISBN: 978-0349120973

Go: An Airline Adventure
by Barbara Cassani
Time Warner Paperbacks (2005) ISBN: 978-0751535600

Trolley Wars: The Battle of the Supermarkets
by Judi Bevan
Profile Books Ltd (2006) ISBN: 978-1861976963

Beyond the Core: Expand Your Market Without Abandoning Your Roots
by Chris Zook
Harvard Business School Press; illustrated edition (2003)
ISBN: 978-1578519514

How To Think Like A Millionaire
by Mark Fisher and Marc Allen
New World Library; 2nd edition (2008) ISBN: 978-1577316435

The Richer Way
by Julian Richer
Richer Publishing; 5th edition (2009) ISBN: 978-0953441525

How the Mighty Fall
By Jim Collins
Random House Business Books (2009)
ISBN: 978-1-8479-4042-1

Good to Great
By Jim Collins
Collins Business (2001)
ISBN: 978-0-712-67609-0

How to Ride a Giraffe
By John Timpson
Caspian Publishing Ltd (2008) ISBN: 978-1-901844-72-6

Sir Alan Sugar – The Biography
By Charlie Burden
John Blake Publishing Ltd ISBN: 978-1-84454-702-9

Appendix 2

A tribute

A big thank you to everyone who has helped, inspired, worked for, supplied or connected with Richard Harpin and his businesses, including all the following and apologies for any missed.

Julie & Paul Ainsworth
Mike Allen
Nick Alexander
Jaime Asua Arrizabalaga
Ricardo Arcos
Bev Aston
Frank Atkinson
Julia Atkinson
Mike Backus
Guy Baculard
Lesley Badger
Jonathan Baggott
Jonathan Bailey
Steve Baker
Atilla Balogh
Derek Bamforth
Alastair Banton
Pete Barnes
Joel Barnett
Christopher Barr
Sandra Basaran
Fred Bassnett
Josie Bates
Mandy Batley
Bob Baty
Christophe Baudin
Steve Beaumont
Kevin Beeston
Andrew Belk
Martin Bennett
Bob Berry
Olivier Besset
Adil Bhatti
Trevor Bish-Jones

Kevin Bishop
Nathan Bishop
Cheryl Black
Andrew Blayze
Tim Blenkin
Simon Blunt
Nigel Boardman
Jackie Boarer
Ed Bolus
Steve Borrowdale
David Bower
Marie Brandt
Richard Branson
Joe Brent
Mark Bridges
Janice Brotherson
Andy Brough
Denise Brown
Guy Bruce
Alan Burton
Lindsay Bury
Ed Byers
Bill Cafferty
Stephane Caine
Nick Cameron
George Campion
Nick Capell
Ian Carlisle
Jesus Carmona
Bob Carson
Tracey Cartwright
James Cashmore
Jarrod Castle
Max Caviet
Hedley Chambers
Russell Chambers
Benoit Chatelain
Ian Cheshire
Ian Chippendale
Michelle Clements
Steve Coathup
Peter Cochrane
Bill Coe
Alan Cole
Mike Cole
Richard Collins
Joanne Cook
Daniel Cooper
Clifford Coote
Panton Corbett
Andy Cornish
Nicholas Cooper
Vivian Corzani
Emma Coulthard
Elaine Crawford
Emma Croom
Gary Cunningham
Tim Davis
Darren Dawes
Allan Dawson
Chris Day
David Dee
Chris de Lapuente
Marc Dench

Frederic Devos
Trevor Didcock
Jane Dixon
Pat Doughty
Siobhan Duffy
Jonathan & Amanda Dunkley
Tony Dunlop
Sandy Dunn
Sebastien Duvanel
Nick Duxbury
Peter Eates
Nigel Edwards
David Elliott
Julie Errington
George Evans
Jo Ewings
Guy Farmer
Jon Farrington
Edward Fitzmaurice
John Flaherty
Pat Flewitt
Jon Florsheim
Ed Foden
Craig Foster
Darren Foster
Johnathan Ford
Alan Fortey
Edward Fox
Antoine Frerot
Ronnie Frost
Steve Garbett
Barry Gibson
Geoff Gillie
Andrew Goodsell
Kevin Gorrie
Richard Gostling
David Graham
Doug Graham
Andrew Grant
Neil Grant
Steve Gray
David Grayson
Mike Green
Paul Greenwood
Richard Gretton
Alan Griffiths
Kareen Griffiths
Stephen Griggs
Andrew Ground
Frank Hall
Gareth Hagan
Bryn Hamer
David Hamid
Simon Hancox
Alison Hanson
Lord Hanson *
John Hardie
Tony Harding
Linda Hardy
Robert Harley *
David Harpin *
Kate Harpin
Philippa Harpin
Stephen Harpin

John Harris *
Anne-Marie Harty
Mike Hartley
Emma Harvey
Helen Harvey
Gareth Haver
Paul Haworth
Mark Hazlewood
Michael Heatley
Angela Heaton
Steve Herbert
Chris Hewitt
Derek Hill
Mike Hilliar
Sian Hirst
Robin Hodgson *
Guy Holland-Bosworth
Steve Hollyoak
Paula Homan
Andrew Honnor
John Houlden
Clive Houlston
Mike Hughes
Rachael Hughes
Alex Hurley
Suzanne Ingham
Ray Irvine
Roger Ivimy
Martin Jackson
Tara Jackson
Ian James
Dawn Jameson
Richard Jenkins
Justin Jewitt
Paul Joesbury
Richard Johns
Wendy Johnson
Ben Jones
Kirran Kaur
Russell Kennedy
Parveen Khan
Jackie Kibbler
Jonathan King
Paul King
John Kirkman
Andy Kirton
Anne Knight
Ronnie Lamb
Heather Lambert
Justin Lambert
Ron Lawrence
Adrian Leadbeater
Simon Lewis
Nick Lobban
Stephen Lord
Geoff Love
Gary Lubner
Ron Lucas
Len Lvovich
John Maclean
Keith Madders
Mark Maddox
Hugh Mainwaring
Stephen Malthouse

Bob Martin
Liz Matthews
Anna Maughan
John Maxwell
Mary McCarthy
Roger McKechnie
Jerome McManus
Sarah McNulty
Myles Meehan
Hugh Meynell
Franco Micelli
Kerry Michael
Alan Middleton
Nick Middleton
Jeremy Middleton
Elena Miguens
Philip Milburn
John Millington
Ben Mingay
Frank Mitchinson
David Moody
Craig Moore
Vanessa Moore
Suzanne Moorse
Mark Morris
Nigel Morris
Sam Morrison
Will Moult
Richard Mowbray
John Moxham
Clare Moy
Karen Mucklin
Ian Muress
Stewart Murray
Sue Myatt
Martin Napper
Jayne Neal
Jon Negri
Cynthia Neptune
Lorraine Nicholls
Mel Nickson
Peter Northwood
Bharat Nalluri
Frederic Obala
Patrick O'Donnell
Hamish Ogston
James Ottewell
Roger Oxtoby
Adrian Page
Sal & Sarah Pajwani
Rick Palmer
Beryl Parker
Tim Parker
Elizabeth Parkes
Nigel Parsons
Ruth Passey
John Peace
Eric Peacock
David Penna *
Nicola Pennells
Tracey Pepper
Jorge Perales
Alasdair Phillips
Stephen Phillips

Richard Pierce
Joyce Piper
Ian Plover
Simon Pook
Mark Poole
David Preston
David Pugh
Steve Purser
Richard Pyne
John Ramdenee
Ian Ramsden
Michael Rauscher
Jackie Reeves
Mike Rhodes
Ian Richards
Emma Richardson
Julian Richer
Simon Robinson
Sue Rogers
Joern Roegler
Lord Redesdale
Cath Rees
Pat Robson
Peter Rowbottom
Alex Rudzinski
Graham Salloway
Olivier Salvat
Steve Sandell
David Sankey
Diane Saunders
John Sansby
Ben Scott
Stuart Senior
Nic Sharp
Richard Shepherd
Ian Shipley
Andrew Sibbald
Jo Simkins
Jonathan Simpson-Dent
Claire Smith
Phil Smith
Patrick Snowball
Sir Martin Sorrell
Jane Sparrow
John Spillane
Debbie Stanton
Brian Strickland
Gwen Stokes
Jeanna Suckling
Lord Sugar
Mike Swallow
Jennifer Synnott
Fran Tansley
Hamish Taylor
Gordon Thew
Emma Thomas
Stuart Thomas
Karen Thorne
Chris Thornley
Steve Throup
Charles Thuku
Ian Tillotson
John Timpson
Claire Tiney

Jerry Toher
Stefan Tournoy
Arnla Tsang
Troy Tucker
Chris Turner
Neil Utley
Jeremy Utton
Barbara Vedrine
Jayne Ventura
Martin Waite
Karen Walker
Paul Walker
Annette Wallace
Carolann Watkins
Chris Webb
Peter Weldon
David Wellings
Ben Wheeler
Brian Whitty
Nick Whitehouse
Trevor Wilkinson
Bankie Williams
Colin Willis
Colin Winsper
Mike Winstone
Eric Woolley
Julian Woolley
Mathew Wootton
Craig Wright
Richard Wrigley
Barry Zyskind

* Deceased

Appendix 3

Sponsors

The following sponsors all significantly support the growth of entrepreneurship in the UK and provide a source of additional help for anyone seeking further advice and guidance.

Apprenticeships – building successful careers

Apprenticeships are an ideal way to gain valuable skills and earn money at the same time. Most of the learning takes place in the workplace, with some time spent off-the-job at college, where apprentices receive training to work towards nationally recognised qualifications. There are over 180 different Apprenticeships available covering an array of sectors and industries including engineering, construction, IT, horticulture, manufacturing, media, hospitality, healthcare and leisure, telecoms and utilities, hospitality, hair and beauty and the public sector.

Any suitably qualified young person aged 16-24 can apply for an Apprenticeship. Apprenticeships can take between one and four years to complete, depending on the level of the Apprenticeship, the ability of the apprentice and the industry sector.

Many apprentices opt for Higher Education when they complete their Apprenticeship and successfully achieve third level qualifications, further enhancing their careers.

Richard is a member of the Apprenticeship Ambassadors Network. The Network is an independent group of senior business leaders from FTSE 100/250 organisations and small and medium sized businesses across the public and private sectors. It is chaired by Sir Roy Gardner, Chairman of Compass Group plc.

Established in 2006 by the Rt Hon Gordon Brown MP (then Chancellor of the Exchequer), the group aims to encourage more employers to take advantage of the Apprenticeship programme because it is a cost-effective way and practical way to build a skilled workforce.

For more information about Apprenticeships please visit **www.apprenticeships.org.uk**

Business of change
Realising Potential

Deloitte.

You've got an idea but how do you make it happen?

Enterprise UK is the national campaign working to give people in the UK the confidence, skills and ambition to be enterprising. Wherever you are on the journey from taking your idea and making it happen, we have a way to encourage and support you.

Through our Take Control Today and Passions into Profit events, we work with people who have great ideas and are only a few steps away from being a business.

Our successful Make Your Mark campaign runs groups, clubs, challenges and offers teacher and student support to get enterprising thinking in schools. Our work in Further Education and our Virgin Media project take this work further.

We run five regional campaign teams and work closely with other regions and the devolved administrations to promote enterprise, run regional awards and support regeneration. Our community networking hub - Enterprising Places Network - connects enterprising minds online and through regional meet-ups.

And if you want to be part of something global, we co-founded Global Entrepreneurship Week; a global movement of enterprising people unleashing their ideas to make the world a more entrepreneurial place and tackling the issues that affect the world's most vulnerable people.

So if you have an idea, and want to make it happen, take the first step and visit our website enterpriseuk.org. There's a community you can join to talk to like minded people, and there's support for everyone including business support organisations, local governments, individuals and you. What are you waiting for?

Welcome to Mediaedge:cia

Mediaedge:cia is a media agency that's part of WPP – the largest advertising and marketing services organisation in the world.

We believe that brands create loyalty by 'actively engaging' consumers. Getting talked about and interacting with consumers builds stronger relationships, which leads to higher sales.

Traditional media (TV, Press, Radio and Outdoor) still has its place but it is also about the integration of Digital, Sponsorship, Entertainment, Retail, Consumer Insight and Return on Investment (ROI) into a campaign.

We work with some great advertisers and their brands – Homeserve, Danone, Lloyds Banking Group, Morrisons, Nintendo, Orange and Paramount.

Around the world, we have 4,500 people working from 250 offices in 84 countries. Here in the UK, we're based in London and Manchester, and support our local communities with mentoring schemes at local schools, raise money for local charities and fund our people to experience local culture.

Our success – *Marketing*'s Media Agency of the Year, a Silver Media Lion at the Cannes Advertising Festival, Grand Prix at the Thinkbox TV Planning Awards and seven prizes at the Hollis Sponsorship Awards (including Agency of the Year) – is attributed to hard work and innovation, attracting talented people and developing successful relationships with some of the world's biggest and most recognisable brands.

If you think you could be part of our success story one day, find out more about us at **www.mecglobal.com**.

Scouting – the Promise of Adventure

There's very little you can't do in Scouting. From taking a flight in a glider or spending a night in the woods to rebuilding a school in Africa, Scouting makes a positive difference not only to young people's lives but also the wider world.

The Scout Association is the UK's largest co-educational youth movement. Offering activities, adventure and personal development opportunities to 400,000 young people aged 6-25, we believe in helping young people experience the outdoors, grow in confidence and reach their full potential.

Each week, thousands of children find out what it means to take a risk, lead a team, make friends and discover that life is as much about possibilities as it is about challenges. Scouting believes in young people. We not only take young people outdoors, but out of themselves.

Skateboarding, climbing, kayaking, camping, sailing, orienteering, cycling, community projects, hiking, grass sledging, potholing... Scouting is all these things, and more. We encourage young people of all backgrounds, male and female, to have self-belief and a voice; to develop physically, intellectually, socially and spiritually. We call this 'everyday adventure.' They just call it fun.

The Scouting formula is simple. Using volunteer adult leaders and basic facilities, Scouting helps young people to develop trust, integrity and a spirit of adventure. In Scouting, we believe that young people develop most when they are 'learning by doing,' when they are given responsibility and think for themselves. Our Scouts are active citizens, some of whom will be tomorrow's leaders.

But Scouting doesn't just happen. To provide everyday adventure to young people, 100,000 adult volunteers donate their time, energy and talents, while adding to their CV and gaining qualifications. Could you do the same?

Join the adventure
To find out how you can be part of it, learn new skills and for flexible volunteering opportunities that fit around you, visit **www.scouts.org.uk/join** or call 0845 300 1818.

The Scout Association is pleased to be working in partnership with Richard Harpin to develop the skills of our Members.

The Scout Association Registered Charity numbers 306101 (England and Wales) and SC038437 (Scotland)

The Prince's Trust is a charity that helps change young lives. We focus on young people aged 14 to 30 who have struggled at school, have been in care, are long-term unemployed or have been in trouble with the law.

Across the UK, there are a million young people who are not in education, employment or training. We believe they all have potential, so we offer simple, practical support to help them unlock their talents.

Since The Trust was established by HRH The Prince of Wales in 1976, we've helped 600,000 young people and we continue to help 100 more each working day.

Through our programmes, we help young people to develop the skills, motivation and confidence they need to set them on their chosen path; whether that's securing an apprenticeship, getting their first job or setting up their own business. The results speak for themselves - more than three in four of the young people we support move into work, education or training.

One of our most successful schemes is our Business Programme - supporting more than 74,000 young entrepreneurs since 1983. Now, more than ever before, we want to give young people as much support as possible to test their business ideas, to develop their skills for enterprise and to launch and sustain successful businesses.

If you're a young person struggling to make your dreams a reality, then we'd love to hear from you. And if you already know what success feels like, then join us on our mission to change more young lives.

princes-trust.org.uk
0800 842 842

Prince's Trust

Notes

If you have a Mind for Business you should use the space on these two pages to write down:

1. The messages and learnings that resonate with you

2. Your personal thoughts and actions